ROSEMARY CONLEY'S

Step by Step

LOW FAT COOKBOOK

ROSEMARY CONLEY'S
Step by Step
LOW FAT COOKBOOK

with Dean Simpole-Clarke

CENTURY

Published by Century in 2005

1 3 5 7 9 10 8 6 4 2

First published in the United Kingdom in 2005 by Century
Random House UK Limited
20 Vauxhall Bridge Road, London SW1V 2SA

Random House Australia (Pty) Limited
20 Alfred Street, Milsons Point, Sydney,
New South Wales 2061, Australia

Random House New Zealand Limited
18 Poland Road, Glenfield
Auckland 10, New Zealand

Random House South Africa (Pty) Limited
Endulini, 5a Jubilee Road, Parktown 2193, South Africa

Random House UK Limited Reg. No. 954009

www.randomhouse.co.uk/century

A CIP catalogue record for this book is available from the British Library

Papers used by Random House UK Limited are natural, recyclable products made from wood grown in sustainable forests. The manufacturing processes conform to the environmental regulations of the country of origin

ISBN 18441 3864 X

Photography by Peter Barry, Clive Doyle, Chris King, Tom Langford
Cover photo by Clive Doyle
Food styling by Dean Simpole-Clarke and Chris Sismore
Designed by Roger Walker

Printed and bound in Germany by Appl Druck, Wemding

Also by Rosemary Conley

Rosemary Conley's Hip and Thigh Diet

Rosemary Conley's Complete Hip and Thigh Diet

Rosemary Conley's Inch Loss Plan

*Rosemary Conley's Hip and Thigh Diet Cookbook
(with Patricia Bourne)*

Rosemary Conley's Metabolism Booster Diet

Rosemary Conley's Whole Body Programme

*Rosemary Conley's New Hip and Thigh Diet Cookbook
(with Patricia Bourne)*

Shape Up for Summer

Rosemary Conley's Beach Body Plan

Rosemary Conley's Flat Stomach Plan

Be Slim! Be Fit!

Rosemary Conley's Complete Flat Stomach Plan

Rosemary Conley's New Body Plan

Rosemary Conley's New Inch Loss Plan

Rosemary Conley's Low Fat Cookbook

Rosemary Conley's Red Wine Diet

Rosemary Conley's Low Fat Cookbook Two

Rosemary Conley's Eat Yourself Slim

Contents

Acknowledgements

This book would not have been possible without the huge contribution made by my chef, Dean Simpole-Clarke. The creation of the recipes and the tips and advice contained throughout the book are primarily down to him. Dean and I have worked together for many years – on TV and on my books and my *Diet & Fitness* magazine – and he is a total star! Thank you, Dean.

No author can create a book like this without the wisdom and talent of an editor who gives their concentrated overview of the whole project as well as attention to detail. Jan Bowmer has edited most of my books and does a superb job both for me and the reader. Thank you, Jan.

Peter Barry has photographed the food for most of my cookbooks over the years and I have always been inspired by his expertise at the photographic sessions. My thanks to Peter, and to Pip, his assistant, for all their hard work in making the food in this book look so delicious.

Thank you also to Clive Doyle for his splendid photography of some of the recipes which have also appeared in my magazine. You have been a joy to work with.

This book would not be here if it were not for my immensely hardworking PA, Melody Patterson, and also Linda Dale. They supervised the collating of photographs, calculated the nutritional information for each of the recipes and generally encouraged me and Dean to get the book completed. Thank you both so much.

My thanks also to Roger Walker, who has done an excellent job in designing the inside pages and making it so easy to follow and inspiring to read. Lastly, thanks to Hannah Black at my publishers, Century, for commissioning it in the first place and for her encouragement and interest along the way, and to sales director Ron Beard for his enthusiasm and support. Thank you all so much.

Useful information

Weight conversions

All weights are given in imperial and metric. All conversions are approximate. Use only one set of measures and do not mix the two. The table below shows the conversions used.

Ounce (oz)	Pound (lb)	Gram (g)
1		25
2		50
3		75
4	¼	115
6		175
8	½	225
16	1	450
	1½	675
	2	1kg

Liquid measures

1 tablespoon	= 3 teaspoons	= ½fl oz	= 15ml
2 tablespoons		= 1fl oz	= 30ml
4 tablespoons	= ¼ cup	= 2fl oz	= 50ml
5 tablespoons	= ⅓ cup	= 2½fl oz	= 75ml
8 tablespoons	= ½ cup	= 4fl oz	= 120ml
10 tablespoons	= ⅔ cup	= 5fl oz	= 150ml (¼ pint)
12 tablespoons	= ¾ cup	= 6fl oz	= 175ml
16 tablespoons	= 1 cup	= 8fl oz	= 250ml (½ US pint)

Note: A UK pint contains 20fl oz

American cup measures can be convenient to use, especially when making large quantities. However, although the volume remains the same, the weight may vary, as illustrated overleaf.

Imperial	American
Flour (plain and self-raising)	**Flour** (all purpose)
1oz	¼ cup
4oz	1 cup
Cornflour	**Cornstarch**
1oz	¼ cup
generous 2oz	½ cup
4½ oz	1 cup
Sugar (granulated/caster)	**Sugar** (granulated)
4oz	½ cup
7½ oz	1 cup
Sugar (icing)	**Sugar** (confectioner's)
1oz	¼ cup
4½ oz	1 cup
Sugar (soft brown)	**Sugar** (light and dark brown)
4oz	½ cup firmly packed
8oz	1 cup firmly packed

Useful measures

1 egg	56ml	2fl oz
1 egg white	28ml	1fl oz
2 rounded tablespoons breadcrumbs	30g	1oz
2 level teaspoons gelatine	8g	¼oz
1oz (25g) granular aspic	sets 1 pint (600ml)	
½oz (15g) powdered gelatine or 4 leaves	sets 1 pint (600ml)	

All spoon measures are level unless otherwise stated.

Wine quantities

Average serving	ml	fl oz
1 glass wine	90ml	3fl oz
1 glass port or sherry	60ml	2fl oz
1 glass liqueur	30ml	1fl oz

Oven temperature conversions

Celsius (Centigrade)	Fahrenheit	Gas Mark	Definition
130	250	½	very cool
140	275	1	cool
150	300	2	warm
170	325	3	moderate
180	350	4	moderate
190	375	5	moderately hot
200	400	6	hot
220	425	7	hot
230	450	8	very hot
240	475	9	very hot

Abbreviations

oz	ounce
lb	pound
kg	kilogram
fl oz	fluid ounce
ml	millilitre
C	Celsius (Centigrade)
F	Fahrenheit
kcal	kilocalorie (calorie)
tsp	teaspoon
tbsp	tablespoon

Equipment and terms

British	American
baking tin	baking pan
base	bottom
cocktail stick	toothpick
dough or mixture	batter
frying pan	skillet
greaseproof paper	waxed paper
grill/grilled	broil/broiled
knock back dough	punch back dough
liquidiser	blender
muslin	cheesecloth
pudding basin	ovenproof bowl
stoned	pitted
top and tail (gooseberries)	clean (gooseberries)
whip/whisk	beat/whip

Ingredients

British	American
aubergine	egg plant
bicarbonate of soda	baking soda
black cherries	bing cherries
broad beans	fava or lima beans
cauliflower florets	cauliflowerets
celery stick	celery stalk
stock cube	bouillon cube
chicory	belgium endive
chilli	chile pepper
British	American
cooking apple	baking apple
coriander	cilantro
cornflour	cornstarch
courgette	zucchini
crystallised ginger	candied ginger
curly endive	chicory
demerara sugar	light brown sugar
essence	extracts
fresh beetroot	raw beets
gelatine	gelatin
head celery	bunch celery
icing	frosting
icing sugar	confectioner's sugar
plain flour	all purpose flour
root ginger	ginger root
self-raising flour	all purpose flour sifted with baking powder
soft brown sugar	light brown sugar
spring onion	scallion
stem ginger	preserved ginger
sultanas	seedless white raisins
wholemeal	wholewheat

Visit www.simpole-clarke.com for unusual ingredients

Introduction

Eating low fat is not only good for your heart and your health, protecting you from a number of diseases, it's good for your figure too. Quite simply, gram for gram, fat contains more than twice the calories of carbohydrate or protein, so cutting down on your intake of fatty foods can help you to lose weight – and keep it off – without resorting to unhealthy, faddy diets.

But low-fat cooking isn't just about losing weight. It's an enjoyable way of eating for everyone which can make a real contribution to a healthier and longer life.

Cooking the low-fat way is quite different from normal cooking methods, but once you get used to it, there will be no turning back. Dishes cooked this way can taste every bit as good as traditional high-fat recipes and it's easier than you think. All it takes is a little know-how and imagination.

In this book you will find all you need to know to get started and learn how to cook your favourite meals the low-fat way as well as discover some fabulous new recipes. The food will taste terrific, it won't take long to prepare and your family will love eating it. Not only that, you will be serving them really healthy food, too, and encouraging them to adopt good eating habits for life. And, if you're having friends round for a meal, you'll find plenty of easy-to-prepare, delicious dishes to grace your supper or dinner party table, with plenty of choices for both meat-eaters and vegetarians, and your guests won't even guess they're low fat.

As well as showing you the special low-fat cooking techniques, there are practical tips on choosing the best utensils and equipment as well as staple ingredients to keep on standby in your store cupboard.

Whether your motivation to cook low fat is for your waistline or your health, this book will help you to get it right and enable you to cook and eat scrumptious food that is healthy AND nutritious at the same time as helping your body to stay healthy and trim.

Enjoy it and happy cooking!

Cooking without fat

To cook the low-fat way there are some basic pieces of equipment you will need, such as non-stick pots and pans and the appropriate utensils to use with them. There are also many stock ingredients that are useful to keep on standby in your larder or store cupboards to enhance your low-fat recipes.

In this section you'll also find basic tips on the special techniques of low-fat cooking and how to minimise the fat content of your dishes without compromising on the taste. It will not take you long to automatically refrain from using olive oil or butter and discover that cooking with wine, garlic and herbs can be a whole new delicious taste experience.

Equipment

Investing in good, solid, hard-wearing equipment will certainly be worthwhile as you find how easy it is to cook the low-fat way. It is worth investing in a top-quality, non-stick wok or frying pan for stir-frying and dry-frying. Try to buy one with a lid if possible, as this helps keep in the moisture and aids thorough cooking of meat and poultry.

Non-stick saucepans are useful for cooking sauces, porridge, scrambled eggs and other foods that tend to stick easily. Always use non-stick utensils with your non-stick pans. Also, treat yourself to a set of non-stick baking tins and trays. Cakes, Yorkshire puddings, scones and lots more dishes can all be cooked the low-fat way.

Choosing the right pan

There are many factors to take into account when selecting pans. Weight, ease of handling and cost are but a few. Heavy-based pans are the most efficient conductors of heat, ensuring a constant quick heat to the food. This style of pan, coupled with a non-stick surface, is definitely the best choice available. Always select the correct-sized pan for the job. Cooking a small quantity in a large pan will cause the pan to burn in areas where the food has no contact. Conversely, too much food in a small pan will result in the food cooking unevenly.

CLEANING A NON-STICK PAN

When cleaning non-stick pans, always soak the pans first to loosen any food still inside. Then wash off with a non-abrasive sponge or cloth. Never use abrasive cleaning materials or abrasive pads, as these will scratch and destroy the non-stick surface. Wash in hot soapy water, preferably with a sponge or soft cloth or custom-made pad for cleaning non-stick pans. Stubborn stains should be soaked overnight.

NON-SCRATCH UTENSILS

Wooden spoons and spatulas, Teflon (or similar) coated tools and others marked as suitable for use with non-stick surfaces are a must. If you continue to use metal forks, spoons and spatulas, you will scratch and spoil the non-stick surface. Treat the surfaces kindly and good non-stick pans will last for years.

Other equipment

There are many other pieces of equipment which are useful in a low-fat kitchen. It is not necessary to have all of the items below unless you cook regularly.

Baking parchment
Aluminium foil
Kitchen paper
Measuring jugs
Kitchen scales
Sieve
Colander
Chopping board
Casserole dishes
Ovenproof dishes
Bowls
Plastic containers with lids
Ramekin dishes
Garlic press
Pastry brush
Whisk (balloon type)
Food processor
Good-quality can opener
Set of sharp knives
Palate knife
Pepper mill
Potato masher (non-scratch)
Pasta spoon (non-scratch)
Slotted spoon (non-scratch)

Non-stick skillet

Non-stick griddle pan

Small non-stick
pancake/omelette pan

Non-stick baking tray

Non-stick utensils

Casserole with lid

Non-stick frying pan with glass lid

Non-stick wok with lid

12-pudding tin

Roasting tin
with rack

4-pudding tin

Non-stick saucepan
with glass lid

Selection of
non-stick baking tins

Lemon squeezer
Grater
Steamer
Wire rack (a grill rack is a good substitute)
Scissors
Multi-surface grater
Zester
Vegetable peeler

The low-fat larder

There are many staple ingredients that are very useful to have in stock. It's best to build up your larder or store cupboard over a period of time to avoid a marathon shopping trip.

Arrowroot
Cornflour
Plain flour

Self-raising flour
Gelatine
Marmite
Bovril
Dried herbs
Tomato ketchup
HP sauce
Fruity sauce
Barbecue sauce
Reduced-oil salad dressing
Balsamic vinegar
White wine vinegar
Cooking spray oil
Black peppercorns
White pepper
Salt
Vegetable stock cubes
Chicken stock cubes
Beef stock cubes
Lamb stock cubes
Pork stock cubes

Long-grain easy-cook rice
Basmati rice
Pasta (various shapes and types)
Oats
Tabasco sauce
Soy sauce
Worcestershire sauce

Fresh items

Garlic
Ginger
Fresh herbs
Lemons
Oranges
Tomatoes
Eggs
Caster sugar
Demerara sugar
Artificial sweetener

Basic cooking techniques

When cooking and preparing low-fat dishes it's important to add moisture and extra flavour to compensate for the lack of oil or fat. Wine, water, soy sauce, wine vinegar, and even fresh lemon juice all provide liquid in which food can be 'fried' or cooked. Some thicker types of sauces can dry out too fast if they are added early on in cooking, so add them later when there is more moisture in the pan.

How to dry-fry foods

One of the key methods used in low-fat cooking is dry-frying, which does away with the need to use oil. The trick is to have your non-stick pan over the correct heat. If it's much too hot, the pan will dry out too soon and the contents will burn. If the heat is too low, you lose the crispness recommended for a stir-fry. Practice makes perfect and a simple rule is to preheat the empty

pan until it is hot (but not too hot) before adding any of the ingredients. Test if the pan is hot enough by adding a piece of meat or poultry. The pan is at the right temperature if the meat sizzles on contact. Once the meat or poultry is sealed on all sides (when it changes colour) you can reduce the heat a little as you add any other ingredients.

Cooking meat and poultry is simple, as the natural fat and juices run out almost immediately, providing plenty of moisture to prevent burning. When cooking minced meat it's best to dry-fry it first and then place the meat in a colander to drain away any fat that has emerged. Wipe out the pan with a wad of kitchen paper to remove any fatty residue before continuing to cook your shepherd's pie or bolognese sauce, or whatever. If you are using onions, always add them after you have dry-fried the meat and wiped out the pan or they will soak up the fat from the meat like a sponge.

Vegetables contain their own juices and soon release them when they become hot, so dry-frying vegetables works well too. When dry-frying vegetables it is important not to overcook them. They should be crisp and colourful so that they retain their flavour and most of their

nutrients. Perhaps the most impressive results are obtained with onions. After a few minutes they go from being raw to translucent and soft and then on to become brown and caramelised.

Good results are also obtained when dry-frying large quantities of mushrooms, as they sweat and make lots of liquid. Using just a few mushrooms produces a less satisfactory result unless you are stir-frying them with lots of other vegetables. If you are using just a small quantity, therefore, you may find it preferable to cook them in vegetable stock.

Occasionally you may wish to add a little cooking spray oil to line your pan or baking tin to aid the cooking or baking of dishes such as 'fried' eggs, fish, cakes, Yorkshire puddings, and so on. Make sure you choose a low-calorie one and use sparingly.

Cutting the fat in meat and poultry

When buying meat or poultry, you can almost halve the fat by selecting low-fat options.

CHOOSE

Lean pork slices, grilled
170 kcal/4g fat per 100g

Sirloin or rump steak, grilled with all fat removed
177 kcal/5.9g fat per 100g

Lamb leg steaks, grilled
198 kcal/9g fat per 100g

Skinless drumsticks, grilled without bone
152 kcal/5.1g fat per 100g

AVOID

Spare rib slices, grilled
292 kcal/19.5g fat per 100g

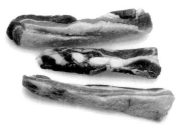

Lean beef steaks, grilled
203 kcal/9.4g fat per 100g

Lamb chops, grilled
231 kcal/13.2g fat per 100g

Drumsticks with skin, grilled without bone, with skin
185 kcal/9.1g fat per 100g

Flavour enhancers

Adding freshly ground black pepper to just about any savoury dish is a real flavour enhancer. You need a good pepper mill and, ideally, you should buy your peppercorns whole and in large quantities. Ready ground black pepper is nowhere near as good.

When cooking rice, pasta and vegetables, add a vegetable stock cube to the cooking water. Although stock cubes do contain some fat, the amount absorbed by the food is negligible and the benefit in flavour is noticeable. Always save the cooking water from vegetables to make soups, gravy and sauces. Again, the fat from the stock cube, divided between however many portions you are serving is very small.

Many herbs can be used to enhance the flavour of foods during cooking.

Here is a quick reference list of ingredients that can be substituted for traditional high-fat ones.

Cheese sauces Use small amounts of low-fat Cheddar, a little made-up mustard and skimmed milk with cornflour.

Custard Use custard powder and follow the instructions on the packet, using skimmed milk and artificial sweetener in place of sugar to save more calories.

Cream Instead of double cream or whipping cream, use 0% fat Greek yogurt or fromage frais. Do not boil.

Instead of single cream, use natural or vanilla-flavoured yogurt or fromage frais.

Cream cheese Use Quark (low-fat skimmed soft cheese).

Creamed potatoes Mash potatoes in the usual way and add low-fat fromage frais in place of butter or cream. Season well.

Roux Make a low-fat roux by adding dry plain flour to a pan containing the other ingredients and 'cooking out' the flour, then add liquid to thicken. Alternatively, use cornflour mixed with cold water or milk, bring to the boil and cook for 2–3 minutes.

Thickening for sweet sauces Arrowroot, slaked in cold water or juice, is good because it becomes translucent when cooked.

Spices

There are many varieties of blended spice mixes to add heat and flavour to all kinds of meat and vegetable dishes. These are great for a quick and easy curry sauce, although many of the individual spice flavours are lost during the blending. Using one or two spices to flavour food rather than a blend adds a more distinctive, delicate flavour.

As spices need to be cooked out in order to obtain the maximum flavour, always start by dry-frying spices in a wok or infusing the spice in the cooking liquor for 2–3 minutes before adding the main ingredient. Here are some great spice combinations:

Cardamom whole pods
Add 4–5 to rice or vegetables during cooking.

Cumin seeds lightly toasted
Add a pinch to cooked carrots or root vegetables.

Coriander seed lightly toasted
Add to salads whole or crush for sauces.

Mustard seed lightly toasted
Add to potatoes or use as a seasoning for fish.

Saffron
Soak in 2 tbsps of boiling water for 5 minutes. Add to cooked rice or stir into yogurt.

Nutmeg
Coarsely grate directly into a hot wok containing vegetables.

Fennel or Fenugreek seeds lightly toasted
Add to cauliflower during cooking.

How to make a low-fat sauce

A normal high-fat creamy sauce is made using equal quantities of fat – butter, oil or meat juices – and flour. They are cooked together to form a roux and then finished with stock, milk or cream. Low-fat sauces are much simpler to make (see recipe below).

SPOT THE DIFFERENCE!

These two sauces look identical but one is made with butter, the other has been made the low-fat way.

Fat savings
600ml (1 pint) low-fat sauce eliminates 50g (2oz) butter = 357 kcal/40g fat.

QUICK THICKENERS

Cornflour or arrowroot may be used to thicken stock or milk for an instant smooth sauce. The powder (4 tsps to 300ml/½ pint liquid) must be mixed first with a little cold liquid (called slaking) then gradually stirred into the preheated stock or milk. Continue cooking, stirring continuously, until the sauce thickens, and boil gently for 2–3 minutes before serving.

Low-fat onion sauce

Makes 600ml (1 pint)

½ **onion, finely chopped**
600ml (1 pint) semi-skimmed milk
2 heaped tbsps cornflour
salt and freshly ground black pepper

1 Preheat a non-stick saucepan. Add the onion and dry-fry until soft.

2 Place the cornflour in a small bowl. Add 2–3 tbsps of the milk and mix with the cornflour.

3 Add the remaining milk to the saucepan and heat.

4 When the milk is hot, gradually stir in the cornflour mixture with a wooden spoon, stirring continuously. As the sauce thickens bring to the boil and simmer for 2–3 minutes. Season to taste.

Enhance your cooking with herbs. Here are some common ones.

coriander

rosemary

thyme

fresh bay leaves

sage

dried bay leaves

lemongrass

dill

chives

parsley

mint

basil

flat leaf parsley

Marinades

You can enhance the flavour of meat, fish and poultry with a low-fat marinade. When grilling, barbecuing or roasting you can either use the marinade to baste the meat or fish before and during cooking or pour the marinade over the meat or fish and leave for a couple of hours or even overnight. The latter method is also ideal when preparing a casserole.

Always add salt during cooking, not before, as it will draw out the juices from the meat if added at the marinade stage.

Try these simple marinades to enhance the flavour of your dishes.

PORK Pineapple juice thickened with tomato purée and a little ground cinnamon.

BEEF Rich soy sauce mixed with a little horseradish sauce and crushed green peppercorns.

LAMB Heated redcurrant jelly or cranberry sauce mixed with a little soy sauce. When cooked, sprinkle with chopped fresh mint.

POULTRY Chopped fresh ginger mixed with fresh orange juice, thickened with a little runny honey.

FISH Toss the fish in a combination of fresh herbs such as chives, parsley and coriander. Drizzle with lemon juice and light soy sauce before cooking.

VEGETARIAN Finely diced red onion mixed with 2 tbsps light soy sauce, 1 crushed garlic clove and 2 tbsps apple sauce.

Stocks

Any chef will tell you that the secret of a good sauce relies on a very good stock. Home-made stock is well worth the effort, as the final flavours are quite different from any convenient stock cube alternatives. If you do decide to make your own stock, make sure you chill it completely. This allows the fat to set, making it easy to remove and discard before adding the stock to your cooking.

There are four basic stocks which are used as a base for many dishes. White stock is pale and light and made from meat and poultry. Unbrowned beef and chicken are excellent for this purpose, while lamb, pork and duck contain much higher levels of fat. Brown stock is made by browning the meat or bones first – you can either dry-fry the meat in a non-stick pan or roast it in a hot oven (the latter method gives a darker colour). Both white and brown stock are then flavoured with root vegetables such as carrots, celery, onions and leeks and left to simmer in plenty of water for 1½–2 hours. A brown stock may be coloured with tomato purée or gravy browning for a deep finish.

Fish stock is quite different and needs careful cooking. The stock should not be allowed to simmer for more than 20 minutes or the bones will make the stock bitter. You can use the bones, heads, skin and tails of any white fish such as sole, brill or plaice. Avoid fatty fish such as mackerel, which will make the stock oily.

Vegetable stock can be made easily by simmering a wide selection of fresh vegetables, taking care not to overpower the flavour with one particular ingredient. You can add tomato purée for additional flavour.

Many recipes in this book use stock cubes for convenience and it is well worth spending a little extra on the better quality ones. Generally, one stock cube will make up with 600ml (1 pint) of water.

Preparing vegetables and herbs

Dicing vegetables

Cubed or diced vegetables may be used as the foundation for casseroles, as a flavouring mixture (mirepoix), raw or cooked in vegetable salads or soups, or as a garnish for consommé (brunoise).

1 Peel the vegetable. Square off the sides, reserving the trimmings for soups or purées. Slice the vegetable vertically, cutting thickly for large dice, thinly for small dice. Stack the slices and cut even strips of uniform thickness.

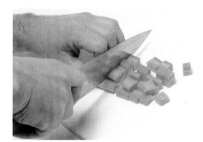

2 Gather the strips together into a pile and slice them evenly crosswise to produce dice of the required size.

Dicing and chopping an onion

An onion can be sliced then cut into even dice, or chopped more finely if called for in the recipe. The thickness of the initial slices will determine the size of the dice.

1 Peel the onion, leaving the root on to hold the onion together.

2 Cut the onion in half and place one half, cut side down, on a chopping board.

3 With a chopping knife, make a series of horizontal cuts from the stalk towards the root. Cut just to the root but not through it.

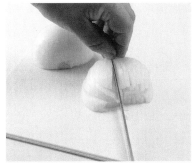

4 Make a series of lengthwise vertical cuts, cutting almost but not quite through the root.

5 Finally, cut the onion crosswise so that it falls into dice. Guide the blade of the knife with your bent fingers. To chop the onion into smaller pieces, continue chopping, bouncing the knife up and down on the board and holding the point down with one end. Continue until the onion is chopped as finely as you like.

Cutting carrots into julienne strips

Julienne strips – fine strips of vegetable the size of a matchstick – cook quickly and make a garnish for many dishes. Juliennes of different coloured vegetables, such as carrots, leeks and turnips, are then mixed for a decorative effect.

1 Peel the carrot and cut a thin strip from one side so that the carrot lies flat on the board.

2 Cut the carrot crosswise into 5cm (2in) lengths, then lengthwise into thin vertical slices.

3 Stack the carrot slices and cut them lengthwise again into strips. For very fine strips, continue cutting, keeping the tip of the knife on the board.

Slicing into a chiffonade

Vegetable leaves such as cabbage, spinach and lettuce may be cut into coarse shreds, known as a chiffonade. Large-leaved herbs such as basil may also be cut this way.

1 Stack the leaves and roll the pile tightly.

2 Slice across the roll to make fine or coarse strips, depending on the leaf you are using.

Preparing peppers

1 Using a sharp chopping knife, cut the pepper in half through the centre.

2 Remove the core and seeds, using a small knife.

3 Tap the pepper to remove any stray seeds and cut away any pith.

4 Slice the pepper or dice as required.

Preparing garlic

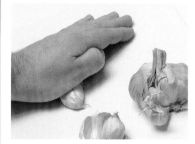

1 Separate the garlic cloves from the main bulb and crush with your hand.

This will make peeling the clove easier.

2 Use a garlic press to squeeze into a paste.

Preparing ginger

1 Place the bulb of ginger on a chopping board. Holding the bulb down with one hand, use a teaspoon to peel away the skin.

2 Using a sharp chopping knife, cut the ginger into fine dice.

How to skin a tomato

1 Using a serrated knife, score a cross on the skin of each tomato.

2 Place in a bowl and pour boiling water over to cover. Leave for 10 seconds then place the tomato immediately into iced water.

3 Remove the skin, cut in half and remove the seeds, using a teaspoon. Chop the flesh as required.

Preparing lemongrass

1 Trim both ends with a sharp knife and remove the dry outer leaves.

2 Chop the lemongrasss finely.

Chopping fresh herbs

There are several ways in which fresh herbs can be chopped. You can use a food processor or a chef's knife, or a two-handled mincing knife, called a mezzaluna. For use as a garnish, herbs can also be shredded into a chiffonade (see page 24).

USING A FOOD PROCESSOR

Strip the leaves from the stalks and put them into the food processor. Turn the machine on and off in short spurts, chopping the leaves to the desired consistency. Take care not to overchop them as this will reduce the herbs to a purée.

USING A MEZZALUNA

Cut through the pile of herbs, rocking the mezzaluna to and fro without lifting it, moving it gradually across the board. Continue chopping until the herbs are the texture you want, either coarse or fine.

USING A CHEF'S KNIFE

1 Strip the leaves from the stalks and pile them on a cutting board.

2 Cut the herbs into small pieces, holding the tip of the blade against the board and rocking the handle up and down. Chop the herbs coarsely or finely, as you wish. Make sure you use a sharp knife or you will bruise the herbs rather than cut them.

Starters

Fresh fruit and salads make simple and practical low-fat starters, but occasionally you want to stretch to something a little more challenging, especially if you're having friends round for a meal. This section offers a tempting selection of stylish and tasty low-fat options that will add colour and interest to your dinner party table. If you're watching your waistline, do keep an eye on the calories, though, or choose a low-calorie main course to follow.

Vegetable spring rolls with dipping sauce

Deep-fried spring rolls are usually dripping in fat. Baked in the oven, they taste great with or without the dipping sauce.

Serves 6 (makes 12)
1 serving 254 kcal/1.7g fat
Preparation time 15 minutes
Cooking time 30 minutes

1 medium onion, finely diced
2 garlic cloves, crushed
1 carrot, finely grated
1 yellow pepper, seeded and
   finely sliced
2 tbsps hot mango chutney
1–2 tsps vegetable bouillon
   powder
150ml (¼ pint) tomato passata
1 egg
3 tbsps skimmed milk
3 sheets filo pastry
paprika to dust

for the sauce
150ml (¼ pint) tomato passata
1 tbsp mango chutney
1 small red chilli, seeded and
   finely chopped
1 tbsp chopped fresh coriander
salt and freshly ground black
   pepper

1 Preheat the oven to 200C, 400F, Gas Mark 6.

2 Preheat a non-stick frying pan; add the onion and garlic and dry-fry until soft. Add the carrot and pepper and continue cooking over a high heat. Add the chutney, stock powder and passata. Simmer gently for 5 minutes until the liquid has reduced to leave a thick paste. Allow to cool.

3 Beat together the egg and milk. Take one sheet of filo pastry and brush with the egg mixture. Using a sharp chopping knife, cut the pastry into 13cm (5in) strips. Place 2–3 tsps of the mixture at one end, fold in 1cm (½in) on both sides of the strip, brush with beaten egg, then roll up like a cigar. Brush with egg, place on a baking tray and dust lightly with paprika. Repeat this process with the remaining sheets of pastry until all the mixture has been used.

4 Bake in the oven for 20–25 minutes until golden brown.

5 Combine all the sauce ingredients, seasoning with salt and black pepper, and place in a small bowl. Serve with mixed salad leaves and the dipping sauce.

Griddled asparagus with fresh lemon and cracked black pepper

Asparagus is delicious cooked over a barbecue or in a griddle pan. Once blanched, it will keep, covered, for 2–3 days in the refrigerator and ready to barbecue or griddle straight from the fridge.

Serves 4
1 serving 88 kcal/3.4g fat
Preparation time 15 minutes
Cooking time 15 minutes

2 bunches (1kg/2lb) fairly thick fresh asparagus
1 vegetable stock cube
1 lemon, quartered
1 tsp cracked black pepper
2 tbsps Parmesan shavings

1 Trim or break the asparagus stems off. Using a vegetable peeler, shave away 5cm (2in) from the base of each stem. Blanch by placing in a pan of boiling water with the vegetable stock cube, and cook for 3–4 minutes.

2 Drain (you can retain the cooking water to use in soup and sauces).

3 Preheat a griddle pan or health grill until hot. Add the asparagus and cook for 2–3 minutes on each side until slightly charred. Squeeze the lemon juice over and season with cracked black pepper.

4 Serve hot with a few Parmesan shavings.

Chicken and chickpea satay

Satay sauce is usually made from peanuts and oil, making it extremely high in fat. This low-fat version has lots of flavour.

Serves 6
1 serving 111 kcal/2g fat
Preparation time 20 minutes
Cooking time 20 minutes

225g (8oz) skinless chicken
   breast
2 tsps mild curry powder
225g (8oz) canned chickpeas,
   drained
1 tsp ground coriander
juice of 1 lemon
2 garlic cloves, crushed
½ tsp salt
2–3 drops Tabasco
150ml (¼ pint) fresh orange
   juice
salt and freshly ground black
   pepper
2 tbsps chopped fresh coriander
a few green grapes to garnish

1 Slice the chicken into thin strips and coat lightly with the curry powder. Thread onto cocktail sticks and place on a non-stick baking tray. Season well with salt and black pepper.

2 Place the chickpeas, ground coriander, lemon juice, garlic and salt in a food processor and blend until smooth. Add Tabasco to taste.

3 Using a knife, spread the mixture over the chicken, coating both sides.

4 Place under a preheated medium/hot grill and cook for 5–6 minutes on each side, turning regularly. Once cooked, drizzle the chicken with the orange juice and place on a serving plate. Sprinkle with chopped coriander and garnish with a few grapes before serving.

Chicken and ham terrine

Traditional terrines and pâtés contain a large proportion of added fat in the form of either butter or dripping. Try this low-fat alternative as a starter or as part of a buffet.

Serves 10
1 serving 198 kcal/7.4g fat
Preparation time 10 minutes
Cooking time 1 hour 30 minutes

450g (1lb) diced chicken breast meat
450g (1lb) gammon, finely chopped
225g (8oz) lean smoked back bacon, finely chopped
150ml (¼ pint) dry white wine
6 green peppercorns, crushed
2 tbsps chopped fresh herbs (parsley, thyme, oregano)
salt and freshly ground black pepper

1 Preheat the oven to 180C, 350F, Gas Mark 4.

2 Mix together all the ingredients in a large bowl. Season well with black pepper and a little salt (the gammon will add plenty of salt during cooking).

3 Press the mixture into a 1kg (2lb) loaf tin or terrine mould. Stand the mould inside a roasting tin and pour sufficient water around to come halfway up the sides of the mould.

4 Cover with foil and bake in the centre of the oven for 1–1½ hours.

5 Remove from the oven, allow to cool, then refrigerate overnight.

6 Serve with salad leaves and lemon wedges.

Coarse duck terrine with spiced nectarines

This lean but luxurious terrine will grace any dinner table. The spiced nectarines can be prepared in advance and stored in the refrigerator for 2 weeks.

Serves 4
1 serving 264 kcal/3.7g fat
Preparation time 10 minutes
Cooking time 2 hours

115g (4oz) skinless duck breast, diced
115g (4oz) lean minced pork
115g (4oz) lean smoked back bacon, finely chopped
1 tbsp dry white wine or sherry
3 juniper berries, crushed
1 tsp vegetable bouillon stock powder
1 tbsp chopped fresh mixed herbs (thyme, oregano, and parsley)
salt and freshly ground black pepper

for the spiced nectarines
4 ripe nectarines
115g (4oz) soft dark sugar
150ml (¼ pint) cider vinegar
2 tsps coriander seeds
½ tsp allspice
zest and juice of 1 lemon
pinch of sea salt

1 Preheat the oven to 180C, 350F, Gas Mark 4.

2 Mix together the terrine ingredients in a large bowl. Season well with salt and black pepper and press into 4 × 50g (4 × 2oz) ramekins.

3 Stand the ramekins in a baking tray and pour in sufficient boiling water to come halfway up the sides of the ramekins. Cover with foil and bake in the centre of the oven for 45 minutes to 1 hour until a skewer inserted comes out clean or temperature probe reaches 75C.

4 Allow to cool, then refrigerate overnight.

5 To make the spiced nectarines, cut the nectarines in half and remove the centre stones.

In a large saucepan dissolve the sugar in the cider vinegar over a low heat. Add the spices, lemon zest and juice and salt.

6 Add the nectarines to the pan, cover and simmer gently for 15 minutes.

7 Remove from the heat and allow to cool, still covered, then pour into a container and refrigerate until ready to use.

8 Thinly slice the terrine and serve cold with the spiced nectarines.

Taramasalata platter

Taramasalata is a creamy dip made from smoked cod roe. This variation uses smoked salmon to create the same creamy texture and flavour but with considerably less fat. It's delicious served with flat breads and freshly cut vegetable sticks.

Serves 4
1 serving 58 kcal/1.3g fat
Preparation time 5 minutes
Cooking time 5 minutes

115g (4oz) smoked salmon
75g (3oz) Quark (low-fat soft cheese)
2 tbsps virtually fat free fromage frais
juice of 1 lemon
salt and freshly ground black pepper

1 Place all the ingredients in a blender or food processor and blend until smooth.

2 Season to taste with salt and black pepper. Chill until ready to serve. Serve with Soft Grain Yogurt Bread (recipe below).

Soft grain yogurt bread

Using a soft grain flour adds texture, as the flour contains flattened grains. Should you find fresh yeast difficult to obtain, substitute dried yeast, or for a yeast-free bread use 2 tsps of baking powder per 225g (8oz) flour.

Makes 8 rolls
1 roll 94 kcal/0.7g fat
Preparation time 5 minutes
Cooking time 20 minutes

225g (8oz) soft grain flour
1 tsp salt
15g (½oz) fresh yeast
2 tbsps low-fat natural yogurt
1 tbsp chopped fresh mint

1 Place the flour and salt in a large mixing bowl. Dissolve the yeast in a small amount of tepid water, sufficient to mix the yeast to a paste.

2 Make a well in the centre of the flour and add the yeast, yogurt and mint.

Using a round-edged knife, draw the mixture together to form a soft dough. If the mixture is too dry, add a little extra water, if too wet, add more flour. Place the dough on a floured board and knead until smooth. Cover with a damp cloth and allow to prove for 20 minutes.

3 After proving, knead again, then divide the dough into 8 equal-sized balls.

4 Using a rolling pin, roll each ball out as thin as possible on a floured surface.

5 Preheat a non-stick frying pan or wok until hot. Add the bread shapes one at a time and cook until they brown on each side. Serve warm.

Mixed pepper bruschetta

Garlic toasts with a rich tomato and pepper relish topping. Assemble just before required and reheat in a low oven as they will go soggy if left for more than 30 minutes.

Serves 4
1 serving 166 kcal/4.4g fat
Preparation time 10 minutes
Cooking time 10 minutes

⅓ **French stick**
2 garlic cloves
6 spring onions, finely chopped
**1 small red and 1 small yellow
    pepper, finely diced**
225g (8oz) tomato passata
**3–4 fresh basil leaves, finely
    shredded**
4 cherry plum tomatoes, sliced
**salt and freshly ground black
    pepper**
salad leaves to garnish

1 Slice the bread diagonally into 8 thick pieces and toast lightly under a hot grill on both sides. Slice 1 garlic clove in half. Rub both sides of the bread with the cut side and place on a baking tray.

2 Preheat a non-stick frying pan and dry-fry the onions for 2–3 minutes until soft. Crush the remaining garlic clove and add to the pan along with the peppers. Cook until soft. Add the passata and simmer over a low heat until most of the moisture has evaporated to leave a paste-like consistency. Allow to cool, then stir in the basil and season to taste.

3 Spread the mixture onto the toasted bread and top with the sliced cherry tomatoes. Return under the grill to brown.

4 Garnish with salad leaves and serve warm.

Prawns wrapped in courgette strips

Large prawns make a good starter or buffet party food. This recipe also works well with scallops or dense fish such as monkfish or fresh tuna.

Serves 6
1 serving 42 kcal/0.7g
   fat
Preparation time 20
   minutes
Cooking time 10
   minutes

2 medium courgettes
18 whole cooked jumbo
   prawns
9 large black seedless
   grapes
4 tbsps freshly
   squeezed orange
   juice
1 tbsp light soy sauce
1 tbsp chopped fresh
   chives
2 small red chillies,
   finely sliced
2 garlic cloves, crushed
1 tsp sesame seeds

1 Using a sharp knife, trim away the top and bottom of both courgettes. Using a vegetable peeler, cut 18 thin strips along the length of the courgettes.

2 Remove the head from each prawn and peel away the outer shell, leaving a little shell near the tail and the tail still attached.

3 Wrap each prawn in a strip of courgette and secure with a cocktail stick. Thread half a black grape onto the stick and place in a shallow container.

4 Combine the remaining ingredients, except the sesame seeds, in a small bowl and spoon over the prawns. Leave to marinate for 20 minutes.

5 Preheat the oven to 190C, 375F, Gas Mark 5. Place the prawns in the oven for 8–10 minutes.

6 Remove from the oven and sprinkle lightly with sesame seeds. Arrange in small stacks on a serving plate.

Jumbo prawns with orange and chilli glaze

If you cannot find large prawns, use the smaller ones, threading 3 or 4 onto
the end of each cocktail stick.

Serves 4
1 serving 60 kcal/1.5g fat
Preparation time 20 minutes
Marinating time 2–3 hours
Cooking time 10 minutes

16 jumbo prawns
zest of 1 orange
1 red chilli, finely sliced
2 tbsps freshly squeezed orange
  juice
1 tbsp light soy sauce
1 tbsp chopped fresh chives
150ml (¼ pint) tomato passata
2 garlic cloves, crushed

1 Peel the prawns, removing the shell and legs. Rinse well and place in the bottom of a shallow dish.

2 Combine the remaining ingredients and pour over the prawns. Leave to marinate in the refrigerator for 2–3 hours.

3 Preheat a non-stick griddle pan until hot. Place the prawns in the pan and cook for 2–3 minutes on each side, basting with the marinade during cooking.

4 Once cooked, press a cocktail stick into each prawn and place on a serving dish.

Smoked salmon pinwheels

Serves 4

1 serving 131 kcal/5g
fat

Preparation time 10
minutes

Cooking time 20
minutes

175g (6oz) salmon fillet
1 vegetable stock cube
175g (6oz) sliced
smoked salmon
juice of ½ lemon
115g (4oz) Quark (low-
fat soft cheese)
1 garlic clove, crushed
6 green peppercorns,
crushed
1 tbsp chopped fresh
dill
freshly ground salt and
black pepper to taste
salad leaves
4 lemon wedges to
garnish (optional)

An attractive first course that looks incredibly difficult to make and yet is actually
quite simple to prepare. Quark is very bland in flavour, so do add plenty of additional
seasoning.

1 Poach the salmon
fillet with the stock
cube for 5 minutes in a
shallow pan containing
sufficient water to cover.
When cooked, lift the fish
from the cooking liquor,
place in a bowl and allow
to cool.

2 Remove the skin and
any bones from the
fish, breaking the fish
apart with a fork. Add the
lemon juice, Quark, garlic,
peppercorns and dill and
mix well, seasoning with
salt and pepper if
required.

3 Place a sheet of
greaseproof paper on
a chopping board and lay
the smoked salmon on
top, overlapping the paper
slightly to make a small
rectangle shape
approximately
20cm × 15cm (8in × 6in).
Carefully spread the
cooked salmon mixture
over, taking it right up to
the edges.
Roll up from the wide
edge like a Swiss roll as
tight as possible then slice
into 8 × 2.5cm (8 × 1in)
discs.

4 Arrange the salmon
pinwheels on a bed of
salad leaves and garnish
with lemon wedges if
desired.

Soups

Who would have thought this simple peasant dish would become the popular dish of today? There are many varieties of soup. Here we've included some vegetable-based, clear soups that are garnished with prawns and noodles or thickened by adding beans and pulses such as red lentils. Others are roux-based and thickened with flour. For a more substantial soup you can purée the ingredients to give a rich thick velvety consistency.

Fresh core ingredients and a good flavoursome stock are the basis of any good home-made soup. These days, fresh stocks are readily available in many shops and supermarkets, as is bouillon stock powder, which simplifies the seasoning of soups and sauces. This instant powder can be sprinkled into the dish during cooking or at the finish, giving you total control over the flavouring.

Some of these recipes call for a little low-fat fromage frais. This should be stirred in just before serving to give a rich, creamy effect. Once you have done this, do not reboil the soup or it will curdle.

Soup can be served as a first course or entrée. Served with some fresh crusty bread, many of these soups also make a tasty, wholesome lunch. Allow 200ml (⅓ pint per serving).

Carrot and parsnip soup with parsley cream

This double soup looks fantastic and tastes delicious. It can be made a day in advance and the basic soup is suitable for freezing, although the parsley cream is not.

Serves 4
1 serving160 kcal/2.7g fat
Preparation time 20 minutes
Cooking time 30 minutes

450g (1lb) fresh young carrots
450g (1lb) young parsnips
2 celery sticks, sliced
2 medium onions, chopped
2 garlic cloves, crushed
2 tsps chopped fresh lemon thyme
1 litre (2 pints) vegetable stock
2 bay leaves
salt and freshly ground black pepper
2 tbsps virtually fat-free fromage frais
1 tbsp chopped fresh parsley

1 Wash the carrots and parsnips well. Remove the tops, peel both vegetables and then slice them. Place in 2 separate saucepans. Divide the celery, onion, garlic and lemon thyme between the 2 pans. Add the vegetable stock and the bay leaves and simmer gently until the vegetables are soft.

2 Remove the bay leaves and liquidise each soup separately until smooth, rinsing out the liquidiser between soups. Return each soup to their original pans to reheat. Adjust the consistency with a little extra stock if required and season with salt and black pepper.

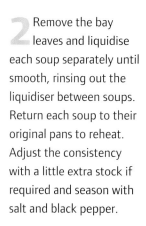

3 Mix together the fromage frais and parsley, and season well with salt and black pepper, adding a little cold water to thin it down.

4 To serve, pour the soups into 2 identically sized jugs and then pour simultaneously into each dish to keep the colours separate. Swirl the parsley cream on top.

Creamy red lentil soup

This is a really easy cook-in-the-pot tasty soup. You can make it in advance and keep in the refrigerator for 5 days.

Serves 4
1 serving 204 kcal/1.3g fat
Preparation time 20 minutes
Cooking time 25 minutes

1 onion, chopped
1 garlic clove, crushed
2 stalks celery, chopped
2 carrots, chopped
2 tsps chopped fresh thyme
1 tsp ground cumin
175g (6oz) dried red lentils
1 litre (2 pints) vegetable stock
1 × 400g can chopped tomatoes
freshly ground black pepper
2 tbsps virtually fat-free
   fromage frais
1 tbsp chopped fresh parsley to
   garnish

1 In a large non-stick saucepan dry-fry the onion until soft.

2 Add the remaining ingredients except the fromage frais and bring to the boil. Reduce the heat and simmer gently for 20 minutes until the lentils are soft.

3 Allow to cool slightly then blend with a stick blender or purée in small batches in a food processor. Thin the soup down with a little extra vegetable stock or water. Reheat in a saucepan as required.

4 Just before serving, remove from the heat, stir in the fromage frais and season to taste with black pepper.

5 Spoon into bowls and garnish with chopped parsley.

Butternut squash soup

Butternut squash, like its name, has a sweet rich buttery flavour which is ideal for a thick creamy soup. If you wish, you can keep the soup chunky by liquidising only half of the soup and mixing it with the unliquidised half.

Serves 4
1 serving 129 kcal/0.8g fat
Preparation time 20 minutes
Cooking time 30 minutes

1kg (2lb) fresh butternut squash
3 celery sticks, sliced
2 medium onions, chopped
1 garlic clove, crushed
2 tsps chopped fresh lemon
** thyme**
1 litre (2 pints) vegetable stock
2 bay leaves
salt and freshly ground black
** pepper**
2 tbsps virtually fat-free
** fromage frais**
chopped fresh chives to garnish

1 Cut the squash in half lengthways, using a large chopping knife. Remove the seeds and peel away the thick skin, using a small knife.

2 Chop the flesh into small pieces. Place in a large saucepan with the celery, onions and garlic and dry-fry over a low heat for 2–3 minutes. Add the thyme, stock and bay leaves and simmer gently until the vegetables are soft.

3 Remove the bay leaves. Place the soup in a liquidiser or blender and liquidise until smooth. Return the soup to the pan, adjust the consistency with a little extra stock if required and season with salt and black pepper.

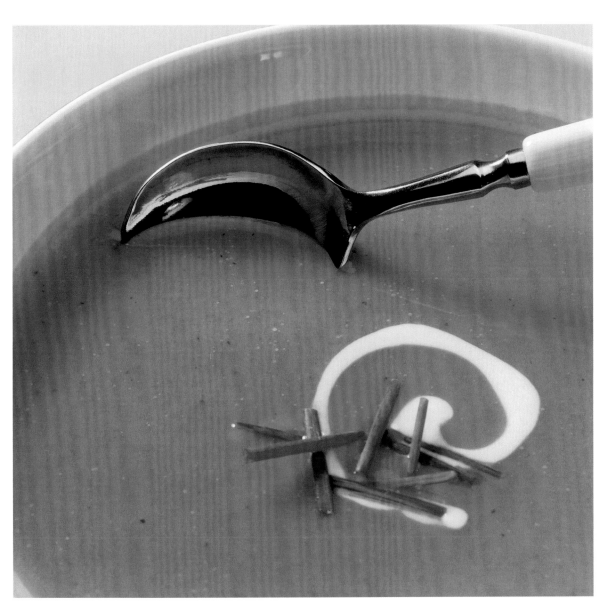

4 Just before serving, remove from the heat and stir in the fromage frais, reserving a little for the garnish. Pour into individual serving bowls. Serve each with a swirl of fromage frais and a pinch of chopped chives.

Soup au pistou

Good, hearty, wholesome fodder. Depending on the salt level in the smoked bacon you may not need to add much stock powder. Vegetarians can omit the bacon and use additional stock.

Serves 4
1 serving 315 kcal/5.3g fat
Preparation time 15 minutes
Cooking time 60 minutes

50g (2oz) white beans, cannellini or haricot, soaked overnight
4 rashers smoked lean back bacon, cut into strips (optional)
4 small shallots, finely chopped
2 garlic cloves, crushed
4 large carrots, diced
2 large baking potatoes (approx. 175g/6oz), diced
2 × 400g cans chopped tomatoes
2 tbsps small pasta shapes
2 tsps chopped fresh oregano
2–3 tsps vegetable stock bouillon powder
black pepper

1 After soaking the beans overnight, rinse well and place in a large saucepan with the bacon, shallots, garlic and carrots.

3 Continue to simmer for a further 25 minutes until the beans are soft. Season well with black pepper and serve hot with crusty bread.

2 Cover with water and bring to the boil. Reduce the heat and simmer gently for 30 minutes, topping up with water as required. Add the potatoes, tomatoes, pasta and oregano. Taste the soup and add sufficient stock powder, adjusting the consistency with more water.

Spicy beef and tomato soup

Served with crusty bread, this hot and spicy soup makes an ideal wholesome
lunch. For a non-spicy version, you can leave out the chilli.

Serves 4
1 serving 212 kcal/6.4g fat
Preparation time 20 minutes
Cooking time 30 minutes

225g (8oz) lean minced beef
1 red onion, finely chopped
2 garlic cloves, crushed
1 red pepper, seeded and finely
**   sliced**
1 × 400g can chopped tomatoes
1 red chilli, seeded and finely
**   chopped**
1 × 400g can red kidney beans
600ml (1 pint) beef stock
salt and freshly ground black
**   pepper**
shredded fresh basil leaves to
**   garnish**

1 Preheat a non-stick frying pan. Add the minced beef to the pan and
dry-fry until browned. Spoon into a sieve and drain away any fat.

2 Add the onion to the pan and cook for 2–3 minutes until soft. Add the
garlic and red pepper and cook for 2–3 minutes more. Return the meat
to the pan.

3 Transfer the mixture to a saucepan and add the tomatoes, chilli, kidney
beans and beef stock, bringing the soup to a gentle simmer. Simmer for
20 minutes to allow the soup to thicken.

4 Season to taste with salt
and black pepper.

5 Just before serving, sprinkle with
shredded basil leaves.

Thyme flavoured white bean soup

Serves 4
1 serving 67 kcal/2.2g fat
Soaking time overnight
Preparation time 15 minutes
Cooking time 60 minutes

**50g (2oz) white beans,
    cannellini or haricot,
    soaked overnight**
**4 rashers smoked lean back
    bacon, cut into strips
    (optional)**
**4 small shallots, finely
    chopped**
2 garlic cloves, crushed
2 celery sticks, chopped
2 tsps chopped fresh thyme
**2–3 tsps vegetable stock
    bouillon powder**
**150ml (¼ pint) skimmed
    milk**
freshly ground black pepper

A delicious, creamy, thick soup. Once finished, this soup is excellent for home freezing. Should you forget to soak the beans you can use canned ones instead.

1 After soaking the beans, rinse well, place in a large saucepan, cover with water and bring to the boil. Simmer gently for 30 minutes.

2 In a separate non-stick pan dry-fry the bacon (if using), shallots, garlic and celery for 5–6 minutes until soft. Place in the saucepan with the beans, and add the thyme and bouillon powder. Reduce the heat and simmer gently for 30 minutes, topping up with water as required.

3 After 30 minutes the beans should be soft. Ladle the soup into a food processor and blend until smooth. Return to the heat and adjust the consistency to your requirements with a little skimmed milk.

4 Season well with black pepper and serve hot with crusty bread.

Prawn noodle soup

This clear soup makes a good spicy starter or light lunch.
Slicing the ginger gives it a tasty bite.

Serves 4
1 serving 121 kcal/2.8g fat
Preparation time 20 minutes
Cooking time 20 minutes

**2 banana or long shallots, finely
    sliced**
1 tsp coriander seed
2 smoked garlic cloves, crushed
**2 tsps finely chopped
    lemongrass**
**small piece fresh ginger, peeled
    and finely sliced**
1 small red chilli, finely sliced
½ tsp ground turmeric
600ml (1 pint) vegetable stock
**50g (2oz) fine egg noodles
    (uncooked weight)**
**115g (4oz) peeled cooked
    prawns, cut in half**
50g (2oz) beansprouts
mint leaves to garnish

1 Preheat a large non-stick pan. Add the shallots and dry-fry until soft. Crush the coriander seed on a chopping board, using the broad side of a chopping knife.

2 Add the coriander to the pan, along with the garlic. Cook for 2–3 minutes, then add the lemongrass, ginger, chilli, turmeric and stir well to combine the spices. Add the stock and bring to the boil. Reduce the heat to a gentle simmer and add the noodles. Cook for 5–6 minutes until the noodles become soft, then add the prawns and continue to cook for 1–2 minutes.

3 Remove from the heat and stir in the beansprouts.

4 Garnish with mint leaves and serve hot.

Cream of leek and mussel soup

Lightly cooked mussels are warmed through in this light, tasty soup starter.

Serves 4
1 serving 126 kcal/
   1.8g fat
Preparation time 20
   minutes
Cooking time 35–40
   minutes

**225g (8oz) cleaned
   mussels
2 garlic cloves, crushed
1 tsp chopped fresh
   thyme
½ glass dry white wine
450ml (¾ pint)
   vegetable stock
4–5 young leeks, finely
   chopped
1 tsp finely grated
   lemon zest
1 tbsp plain flour
450ml (¾ pint)
   skimmed milk
2 bay leaves
1 tbsp chopped fresh
   parsley
salt and freshly ground
   black pepper**

1 Wash the mussels well and place in a saucepan. Add the garlic, thyme, wine and stock. Cover with a lid and place over a high heat for 5–6 minutes until all the shells have opened.

2 Remove the pan from the stove. Using a slotted spoon or fork, lift out the mussels into a bowl, drain, and reserve the cooking liquor.

3 In a separate non-stick pan dry-fry the leeks until soft with no colour. Add the lemon zest and 3 tbsps of the cooking liquor. Sprinkle the flour over and cook out for 1 minute, stirring well with a wooden spoon. Gradually add the remaining stock along with the skimmed milk. Add the bay leaves and gently simmer for 20–25 minutes until the soup has slightly thickened.

4 Meanwhile, remove the mussels from their shells. Just before serving, stir in the mussels and chopped parsley. Adjust the seasoning and serve with crusty bread.

Meat

With farmers breeding leaner cuts of meat, low-fat cooking has never been easier. Check out the extra-lean meat packs or reduced-fat cuts on offer.

There are endless selections of prepared meats and choosing the right cut can sometimes be quite daunting. The key rule is to choose clean, clear-coloured meat that is not dull and grey in appearance and certainly without dried edges.

Small cuts should be evenly sliced or diced into uniform-sized pieces to make sure they cook properly at the same time.

Organic or free range meat may seem expensive, but the flavour and texture will be far superior.

Meat should always be stored, wrapped, in the coldest part of the refrigerator. Most small cuts and mince are best used within one or two days of purchase. Generally, red meat tends to keep better than white, but if in doubt, throw it out!

Dry-frying

The key to dry-frying is to make sure you preheat your frying pan or wok until it is hot enough to cause a piece of meat to sizzle when added to the pan. This seals in the natural juices of the meat and makes the flesh tastier.

Try sprinkling plenty of freshly ground black pepper into the pan before adding the rest of the meat.

The same principle applies whether you are cooking a gourmet recipe or a quick-and-easy one using a jar of branded stir-fry sauce. All cuts of meat and poultry are suitable for dry-frying.

How to dry-fry minced beef

1 Heat a non-stick pan or wok until it is hot, and sprinkle liberally with freshly ground black pepper. Add the raw mince and distribute evenly across the base.

2 Toss the mince to cook on all sides to release the fat, then continue cooking until the mince totally changes colour.

3 Place a sieve over a bowl and pour the mince into the sieve. Shake and stir the beef to remove as much fat as possible.

4 This is the fat extracted from 450g (1lb) mince – it should be thrown way.

5 Using a thick wad of kitchen paper, wipe out the pan to remove the fat, taking care not to burn yourself. Do not wash the pan at this stage.

6 Return the pan to a moderate heat and add 1 finely chopped onion and 1 crushed garlic clove. Stir the onion and garlic until they begin to soften.

7 When the onion starts to go brown, return the mince to the pan. At this stage add any diced vegetables, such as carrots, and your cooking sauce ingredients.

8 For cottage pie, add 300ml (½ pint) water to the pan with 3 tsps low-fat gravy granules. Cook for 10 minutes to allow the gravy to thicken.

Cottage pie with leek and potato topping

Serves 4
1 serving 327 kcal/6.2g fat
Preparation time 30 minutes
Cooking time 30 minutes

for the topping
675g (1½lb) potatoes, chopped
2 leeks, sliced
2 tbsps skimmed milk
salt and freshly ground black
    pepper

for the mince
450g (1lb) lean minced beef
1 onion, chopped
2 carrots, chopped
2 tbsps plain flour
300ml (½ pint) beef stock
1 tbsp tomato purée
1 tbsp mixed dried herbs
salt and freshly ground black
    pepper to taste

1 Preheat the oven to 190C, 375F, Gas Mark 5.

2 Boil the potatoes until softened, adding the leeks 5 minutes before the end of cooking.

3 Preheat a non-stick frying pan, add the mince and dry-fry for 3–4 minutes. Remove the mince from the pan and drain. Discard the liquid and put the meat to one side. Wipe out the pan, then return the meat to the pan

4 Add the onion and carrots to the pan and stir in the flour. Gradually add the stock, tomato purée and dried herbs. Bring to the boil and stir until thickened. Season with salt and black pepper and transfer to an ovenproof dish.

5 Drain the potatoes and leeks, and mash with a little skimmed milk. Season to taste. Arrange on top of the mince mixture, pressing the mash down with the back of a fork.

6 Bake in the oven for 25 minutes until crisp and golden on top.

Chilli beef pizza

Serves 4
1 serving 384 kcal/8g fat
Preparation time 10 minutes
Cooking time 35 minutes

225g (4oz) lean steak mince
1 medium onion, finely chopped
2 garlic cloves, crushed
2 beef stock cubes
1 red pepper, seeded and finely
   chopped
1 tbsp chopped fresh oregano
1 × 400g can chopped tomatoes
1–2 fresh red chillies, sliced
50g (2oz) low-fat Cheddar
   cheese, grated
a few basil leaves, shredded

for the dough
225g (8oz) strong white bread
   flour
1 tsp salt
15g (½oz) fresh yeast or 2 tsps
   dried yeast
150ml (¼ pint) warm skimmed
   milk

This giant-sized pizza offers a really good portion. If you wish, divide the dough into individual pizzas and freeze complete with the topping.

1 Preheat the oven to 200C, 400F, Gas Mark 6. Preheat a non-stick frying pan.

2 Add the mince to the frying pan and dry-fry until lightly browned. Pour the meat into a sieve to drain away the fat.

3 Remove the pan from the heat, wipe out the pan with kitchen paper. Return the pan to the heat, add the onion and garlic to the pan and dry-fry for 2–3 minutes until soft. Return the meat to the pan and crumble the stock cubes on top. Add the red pepper, oregano and chopped tomatoes. Simmer gently for 20–25 minutes until the sauce has thickened and the meat is tender.

4 While the beef is cooking, place the flour and salt into a large mixing bowl and make a slight well in the centre. Dissolve the yeast in the milk, add to the flour and mix together with the blade of a round-ended knife, adding more liquid if required. Turn out onto a floured surface and knead well to form a soft dough. Cover with a damp cloth for 10 minutes.

5 Knead the dough again. Roll it out into a large circle and place on a non-stick baking tray or pizza pan. Spoon the beef mixture over, leaving a border around the edge. Scatter with the sliced chillies and cover with grated cheese.

6 Bake near the top of the oven for 20 minutes.

7 Just before serving scatter with shredded basil. Serve hot.

FACTS ABOUT MINCE

Minced beef is generally meat taken from the neck and flank area of beef. These cuts are renowned for having a high proportion of fat. Recent trends have called for leaner minced beef using other cuts of beef, including minced steak cuts that have less fat distributed throughout the meat.

Nutritional values based on 115g (4oz)

Regular minced beef	259 kcal	18g fat	23g protein
Lean minced beef	200 kcal	10.5g fat	25g protein

Chilli beef enchiladas

Tortillas form the base to this Mexican feast. If you wish, you can replace the beef with minced chicken or pork, and a good vegetarian filling is roasted vegetables.

Serves 4
1 serving 351 kcal/13.4g fat
    excluding tortilla
Preparation time 10 minutes
Cooking time 35 minutes

450g (1lb) lean steak mince
2 medium onions, finely
    chopped
3 garlic cloves, crushed
2 beef stock cubes
1–2 fresh red chillies, chopped
2 red peppers, seeded and finely
    chopped
1 tbsp chopped fresh flat leaf
    parsley (oregano)
1 × 400g can chopped tomatoes
300ml (½ pint) tomato passata
300ml (½ pint) skimmed milk
3 tsps cornflour
4 Navajo Tortillas (see recipe
    opposite)
50g (2oz) low-fat Cheddar
    cheese, grated
salt and freshly ground black
    pepper

1 Preheat the oven to 200C, 400F, Gas Mark 6.
Preheat a non-stick frying pan.

2 Add the mince to the frying pan and dry-fry until lightly browned. Pour the meat into a sieve to drain away the fat.

3 Remove the pan from the heat, wipe out the pan with kitchen paper. Return the pan to the heat, add the onions and garlic and dry-fry for 2–3 minutes until soft.

3 Return the meat to the pan and crumble the stock cubes over. Add the chillies, peppers, oregano and both chopped and passata tomatoes. Simmer gently for 20–25 minutes until the sauce has thickened and the meat is tender.

4 In a separate pan heat the milk. Slake the cornflour with a little cold water and whisk into the milk. Stir as the sauce thickens, seasoning well with salt and black pepper.

5 Take a tortilla and place a line of the beef mixture down the centre. Roll up and place in an ovenproof dish. Repeat with the remaining tortillas, placing any meat mix on top of each. Pour the sauce over and sprinkle with grated cheese.

6 Bake in the oven for 20–25 minutes until golden brown. Serve with red pepper salsa and mixed green leaves.

Navajo tortillas

Makes 8
1 tortilla 209 kcal/0.9g fat
Preparation time 5 minutes
Cooking time 20 minutes

450g (1lb) soft white flour
1 tsp fine salt
2 tsps baking powder
2 tsps English mustard powder
2 tbsps chopped fresh coriander
300ml (½ pint) skimmed milk
a little vegetable oil

These simple flat breads are delicious eaten straight from the pan, but for ease cook them in advance and reheat for 4-5 minutes in a low oven. The mustard powder adds a golden colour as well as flavour.

1 Sieve all the dry ingredients into a large mixing bowl. Add the coriander and mix in. Using a flat-edged knife, make a well in the centre of the flour and slowly add sufficient milk, bringing the mixture together with the knife to form a soft dough.

2 Divide the dough into 8 equal balls. Using a rolling pin, roll out each ball on a floured surface into a circle, getting the dough as thin as you can. Stack the breads, dusting in between with flour.

3 Preheat a large non-stick frying or griddle pan until hot. Add a small amount of vegetable oil then wipe out the pan with a thick pad of kitchen paper.

4 Cook the tortillas in the hot pan for approximately 1 minute each side. Don't worry if the bread has black markings as this will add flavour. Stack the breads onto a warm plate and serve or reheat as required.

Thai pork

An easy way to liven up the simplest of pork dishes. Make sure you slice the pork fillets into thin strips to ensure they cook quickly and evenly.

Serves 4
1 serving 254 kcal/
    5.9g fat
Preparation time 10 minutes
Cooking time 15 minutes

450g (1lb) lean pork fillets, cut into strips
1 medium red onion, finely sliced
1 red pepper, seeded and sliced
2 small courgettes, sliced
115g (4oz) chestnut mushrooms, sliced
1 tsp chopped fresh ginger
1 tbsp reduced-salt soy sauce
1 tbsp hot mango chutney
2 tsps finely chopped lemongrass
salt and freshly ground black pepper

1 Preheat a non-stick wok or frying pan. Add the pork strips and season well with salt and black pepper. Dry-fry for 5–6 minutes or until just cooked.

2 Add the onion, red pepper and courgettes and dry-fry for 2–3 minutes, tossing the vegetables in the wok or pan. Add the mushrooms and ginger and mix well.

3 Mix together the soy sauce, mango chutney and lemongrass and add to the pan, coating the meat and vegetables.

4 Serve immediately on a bed of noodles.

Tomato, orange and chilli glazed pork

Choose lean pork steaks with a minimum of fat. These tasty slices can also be barbecued for extra flavour, with the sauce served alongside.

Serves 4
1 serving 348 kcal/10g fat
Preparation time 10 minutes
Cooking time 20 minutes

4 lean pork steaks
1 medium red onion, finely chopped
2 garlic cloves, crushed
1 small red chilli, finely sliced
1 red pepper, seeded and diced
600ml (1 pint) tomato passata
2 tbsps Seville marmalade
2 tsps vegetable stock powder
1 tbsp chopped fresh mixed herbs
salt and freshly ground black pepper
1 large tomato, sliced, to garnish

1 Preheat a non-stick pan. Trim any traces of fat from each pork slice. Using a rolling pin, beat each steak into a thin slice and season generously with salt and black pepper.

2 Seal the slices in the hot pan on both sides, then remove and keep warm.

3 Add the onion, garlic, chilli and red pepper to the pan. Cook quickly over a high heat to soften. Add the tomato passata, marmalade, stock powder and herbs and stir well.

4 Return the pork to the pan. Cover and simmer for 5–6 minutes to allow the pork to cook through.

5 Garnish with tomato slices and serve immediately with a selection of fresh vegetables.

Grills and griddles

Grilled lamb steaks with redcurrant jelly

Serves 4
1 serving 327 kcal/15g
   fat
Preparation time 10
   minutes
Cooking time 20
   minutes

**4 lean lamb leg steaks
   or chops
4 tbsps dry sherry
2 garlic cloves, sliced
4-5 sprigs fresh
   rosemary, chopped
2 tbsps redcurrant jelly
pinch of paprika
2 tsps arrowroot
salt and freshly ground
   black pepper**

1 Remove all the fat from the lamb steaks with a sharp knife and place the steaks in a shallow container. Season with salt and black pepper.

2 Combine the remaining ingredients, except the arrowroot, in a small bowl and mix well. Pour over the lamb and turn the steaks over, coating both sides.

3 Preheat the grill to high. Cook the steaks on a wire rack for 8–10 minutes on each side, basting with more glaze if required.

4 Pour the remaining glaze into a small saucepan and heat. Slake the arrowroot with a little cold water and gradually add to the glaze, stirring well. Place the lamb steaks on a serving dish and pour the hot sauce over. Serve with potatoes and a selection of fresh vegetables.

Griddled beef with salsa verde

A simple dish that looks stunning. Make the salsa in advance and store in the refrigerator until ready to serve.

Serves 4
1 serving 252 kcal/9g fat
Preparation time 10 minutes
Cooking time 10 minutes

4 lean fillet steaks
2 tsps Dijon mustard
4 large field mushrooms
1 wineglass red wine
salt and freshly ground black
    pepper

for the salsa
1 small green pepper, finely
    chopped
5 spring onions, finely chopped
1 tbsp chopped fresh mint
1 tbsp mild mango chutney
zest of 1 lemon

1 Season the steaks with salt and black pepper and lightly spread with the mustard. Preheat a non-stick griddle pan until hot. Add the steaks and cook for 2–3 minutes on both sides. Remove the steaks from the pan, cover with foil and allow to rest for 2 minutes on a chopping board.

2 Meanwhile, add the mushrooms and the wine to the pan and cook for 2 minutes until the mushrooms are soft and the wine reduced.

3 Combine the salsa ingredients and place in a small serving bowl.

4 Place the mushrooms on a serving dish and place a steak on top of each one. Pour the juices from the pan over the top. Serve with the salsa.

Casseroles

Most lean meats are suitable for low-fat casseroles. The key to success is in the preparation – sealing the meat, dry-frying the vegetables and optimising on the combination of flavours. Most casseroles can be prepared well in advance and can be frozen very satisfactorily.

Flavourings for casseroles

Wine – red and white
Wine has been a cooking medium for centuries. As well as flavouring the finished sauce it also has tenderising properties.

Orange peel
This is used in Moroccan and other cuisine to add a citrus flavour. Good with red meat.

Preserved lemons
Lemons preserved in a strong salt brine become more mellow in flavour. Delicious with chicken or pork.

Cinnamon sticks
These are used in moderation to add spice and character to many meat- or vegetable-based dishes.

Garlic, shallots, onions
These all form the base to a good casserole. Fresh garlic has a more robust flavour than dried. Shallots and red onions tend to be slightly sweeter in flavour than white onions.

Bouquet garni
Herbs wrapped together to form a bundle are added to enhance the flavour of the casserole.

HOW TO MAKE A BOUQUET GARNI

A bouquet garni is a collection of fresh herbs tied together with string. It is added to casseroles to flavour the sauce.

Two bay leaves form the outer part, sandwiching fresh thyme or parsley in between. Tie them all together, using string, which makes it easier to retrieve and remove when the dish is finished.

A prepared bouquet garni can be bought in supermarkets. These are made on the same principle, using dried herbs in a perforated casing.

Equipment

A good casserole dish should feature on your 'must have' list of kitchen equipment.

Electric slow cooker

Non-stick casserole pan

Le Creuset cast iron casserole

Non-stick spoons and spatulas

Ceramic casserole with lid

HOW TO CLEAN YOUR CASSEROLE DISH

Because of the length of time involved in cooking a casserole, a little food may become baked on the inside. The simplest way to clean a casserole dish is to leave it soaking overnight. The food particles should then be easy to remove.

Beef bourguignonne

Serves 6
1 serving 500 kcal/15g fat
Preparation time 15 minutes
Cooking time 40–55 minutes

1kg (2lb) lean braising beef
2 medium onions, finely
    chopped
2 garlic cloves, crushed
2 tsps chopped fresh thyme
2 beef stock cubes dissolved in
    300ml (½ pint) water
2 tbsps plain flour
1 bottle red wine
300ml (½ pint) tomato passata
4 large carrots
3 celery sticks, cut into 5cm
    (2in) batons
175g (6oz) button mushrooms
20 baby onions, peeled
salt and freshly ground black
    pepper
bouquet garni
chopped fresh parsley to garnish

1 Preheat the oven to 180C, 350F, Gas Mark 4. Cut the beef into 2.5cm (1in) dice, removing all fat and sinew.

2 Season the beef with salt and freshly ground black pepper and place in a preheated, non-stick pan.

3 Seal the meat on all sides in small batches until lightly browned. Remove from the pan and set aside.

4 Add the onions, garlic and thyme to the pan and cook gently for 2–3 minutes until soft.

THICKENING AGENTS

Even though most casseroles use flour in their initial making, sometimes it may not be sufficient to thicken the finished dish. Just add 2–3 tsps of cornflour or arrowroot mixed with cold water to a smooth paste before the end of cooking and simmer for 2–3 minutes. Add it gradually while continuously stirring the casserole.

5 Add 2 tbsps of stock, then sprinkle the flour over, stir well and cook for a further minute to 'cook out' the flour.

6 Gradually stir in the remaining stock along with the wine and tomato passata.

7 Cut the carrots into 4cm (1½in) lengths. Using a small sharp knife, carefully peel away the outside skin to form the carrot pieces into barrel shapes.

8 Add the carrots, celery, mushrooms and baby onions to the sauce.

9 Place the beef in the bottom of a large casserole dish and pour the sauce and the vegetables over.

10 Add the bouquet garni and cover with a lid. Place in the oven for 35–40 minutes until the sauce has reduced.

CHEF'S TIP

Easy peeling
To ease the peeling of small shallots, cover them with boiling water for 1 minute before draining. They will then peel easily.

11 Remove the bouquet garni, and garnish with parsley before serving.

Lemon pork with capers

A succulent pork dish that combines unusual flavours.
This recipe also works with chicken or turkey steaks.

Serves 4
1 serving 473 kcal/9.7g fat
Preparation time 20 minutes
Cooking time 50 minutes

1kg (2lb) pork fillet
2 red onions, finely chopped
2 garlic cloves, crushed
2 small celery sticks, sliced
300ml (½ pint) vegetable stock
1 tbsp plain flour
2 tsps chopped fresh lemon
   thyme
1 cinnamon stick
2–3 pieces lemon peel
750g (1¾lb) tomato passata
½ wineglass dry white wine
115g (4oz) capers
2 tbsps chopped fresh flat leaf
   parsley
salt and freshly ground black
   pepper

1 Preheat the oven to 200C, 400F, Gas Mark 6. Preheat a non-stick frying pan or wok.

2 Cut the pork into chunky discs and season well with salt and black pepper. Pan-fry each piece over a high heat to seal the meat, and place in an ovenproof dish.

3 Add the onions, garlic and celery to the pan and soften. Add 2–3 tbsps of stock to the pan, then sprinkle the flour over. Mix well, and 'cook out' the flour for 1 minute.

4 Gradually stir in the remaining stock and add the remaining ingredients, except the parsley. Bring the sauce to the boil to allow it to thicken, then pour it over the pork. Cover with foil and place in the centre of the oven for 30–35 minutes.

5 Remove from the oven and stir in the parsley. Serve with a selection of fresh vegetables.

Smoked ham and mushroom coddle

Coddle refers to an old recipe that uses potatoes to cover the main dish which is then cooked in the oven. This recipe uses a creamy low-fat ham and mushroom mix. For a vegetarian version replace the ham with a selection of frozen vegetables or canned beans.

Serves 4
1 serving 266 kcal/3.9g fat
Preparation time 10 minutes
Cooking time 35–40 minutes

300ml (½ pint) skimmed milk
1 tbsp vegetable stock powder
   or 1 vegetable stock cube
4 tsps cornflour
1 tbsp Dijon mustard
50g (2oz) low-fat Cheddar,
   grated
115g (4oz) thinly sliced smoked
   ham, cut into strips
1 tbsp chopped fresh chives
4 medium baking potatoes,
   thinly sliced
1 tbsp light soy sauce
salt and freshly ground black
   pepper

1 Preheat the oven to 190C, 375F, Gas Mark 5.

2 In a saucepan, heat the milk with the stock. Dissolve the cornflour in a little cold water and stir into the sauce. Stir continuously as the sauce thickens, then reduce the heat and simmer for 2–3 minutes.

3 Stir in the remaining ingredients, except the potatoes, and season well with salt and black pepper.

4 Pour into the bottom of an ovenproof dish. Cover with the sliced potatoes and drizzle with the soy sauce.

5 Place near the top of the oven and bake for 35–40 minutes until golden brown. Serve hot with a selection of fresh vegetables.

Lamb and pepper crumble

The crunchy topping in this recipe can be used on many different foods such as fish or chicken. It's a good way of using up stale bread.

Serves 6
1 serving 377 kcal/15g fat
Preparation time 10 minutes
Cooking time 45 minutes

1kg (2lb) lean diced lamb
1 medium red onion, finely
  chopped
2 garlic cloves, crushed
1 red pepper, seeded and finely
  chopped
600ml (1 pint) tomato passata
2 tsps vegetable stock powder
  dissolved in 300ml (½ pint)
  water
1 tbsp chopped fresh mixed
  herbs
115g (4oz) fresh breadcrumbs
2 tbsps chopped fresh mint
2 tbsps cranberry sauce
salt and freshly ground black
  pepper

1 Preheat the oven to 200C, 400F, Gas Mark 6. Preheat a non-stick pan.

2 Trim away any traces of fat from the lamb, then season generously with salt and black pepper. Seal the meat in the hot pan on all sides. Add the onion, garlic and red pepper to the pan. Cook quickly over a high heat to soften. Add the tomato passata, stock and herbs, stirring well.

3 Cover and simmer for 20 minutes to allow the lamb to cook through.

4 Meanwhile, place the breadcrumbs on a baking tray and grill under a medium heat, turning them with a spatula, until well toasted.

5 When toasted, place in a mixing bowl, add the chopped mint and mix in the cranberry sauce.

6 Place the lamb in the bottom of an ovenproof dish and scatter the crumble on top. Bake in the oven for 20 minutes.

7 Serve with a selection of fresh vegetables.

Lamb and pearl barley casserole

It is very important the lentils and beans are soaked overnight as they cannot be cooked directly from their dried state.

Serves 4
1 serving 402 kcal/10.5g fat
Preparation time 15 minutes
Cooking time 1 hour 45 minutes

2 medium onions, diced
2 garlic cloves, crushed
450g (1lb) lean diced lamb
4 carrots, diced
1 large turnip, diced
450g (1lb) small charlotte
    potatoes
2 celery sticks, chopped
1 litre (2 pints) meat stock
bouquet garni
50g (2oz) green lentils, soaked
    overnight
25g (1oz) haricot beans, soaked
    overnight
25g (1oz) pearl barley
salt and freshly ground black
    pepper
2 tbsps chopped fresh parsley

1 Preheat a non-stick pan, add the onions and garlic and dry-fry for 2–3 minutes until soft.

2 Add the lamb, seasoning well with salt and black pepper, and continue to cook over a high heat until well sealed.

3 Transfer to a large casserole dish and add the remaining vegetables, the stock and the bouquet garni.

4 Rinse the lentils, beans and pearl barley well and add to the casserole.

5 Cover and simmer gently for 1 hour or until the meat is tender, topping up with additional stock if required.

6 Remove the bouquet garni and, just before serving, sprinkle with fresh parsley.

Marinated venison with port and redcurrants

Venison is a lean meat that is generally lower in fat than other red meats. Its flavour is similar to beef. Steaks can be cooked using a quick method such as grilling, while other cuts are suitable for slow braising.

Serves 4
1 serving 277 kcal/2.5g fat
Preparation time 40 minutes
Cooking time 20 minutes

450g (1lb) lean venison fillet
2 garlic cloves, crushed
few sprigs of fresh rosemary
300ml (½ pint) port wine
50g (2oz) fresh redcurrants
1 tbsp redcurrant jelly
1 tbsp cornflour
1 tbsp chopped fresh flat leaf parsley
salt and freshly ground black pepper

1 Cut the venison into 4 steaks and place in a shallow dish. Sprinkle with the garlic and rosemary and season with salt and black pepper. Pour the port wine over and leave to marinate for 30 minutes.

2 Remove the venison from the marinade and place on a grill tray. Cook under a hot grill or in a griddle pan for 5–6 minutes on each side.

3 Pour the marinade into a small saucepan, add the redcurrants and redcurrant jelly, and heat gently.

4 Slake the cornflour with a little water and add to the sauce. Stir well until the sauce starts to thicken, adding the chopped parsley.

5 Arrange the venison steaks on a serving dish and pour the sauce over.

Mention roast beef, Yorkshire pudding and roast potatoes, and most people think of it as indulgent and fattening – and, indeed, cooked the traditional way, it is. Using non-stick utensils, herbs and simple flavourings, your roast dinner can taste just as delicious as a high-fat one.

The term roasting applies to a quick method of cooking at a high temperature. The meat or joint sits on a rack to allow the maximum surface area to be exposed to the heat and for the fat to drip away.

It is important that the joint sits above the roasting tin, and not in it, to prevent it from stewing in the juices and the fat it produces during cooking. Spit roasting or rotisserie is the perfect roasting method, as the meat turns evenly during cooking and is evenly cooked on all sides.

Equipment

KNIVES

A good carving knife is essential to add ease to slicing both meat and poultry. Generally, a long slender blade is necessary to provide smooth, even slices using the whole length of the knife during carving.

Sharpening steel

Carving knife

Carving fork

Look for strongly constructed knives where the blade is forged into the handle and not a separate attachment.

SHARPENING KNIVES

Sharpening knives regularly keeps the edge in good condition. Electric sharpening devices tend to wear the blade down, so choose a wet stone disc or, better still, the traditional steel, a rod-shaped textured file made of hardened steel or more modern ceramic versions.

To sharpen a knife, hold the steel in one hand and the knife in the other as shown. Run the blade of he knife down, using the length of the blade on both sides of the knife.

FOOD THERMOMETER

Using a food thermometer is one of the most reliable ways of testing when a joint is cooked to a suitable and safe degree. Some are designed with a metal skewer and are reasonably inexpensive. More sophisticated digital types cost more.

How to prepare a joint for roasting

1 Prepare the joint, removing all surface fat.

2 Place the onion, carrot, celery and herbs in the bottom of a roasting tin. Pour in the water.

3 Place a roasting rack over the non-stick roasting tin, and place the joint on top. Season well with salt and black pepper.

4 Cover with foil and place in a preheated oven.

5 Baste the joint by spooning the pan juices over it, using a non-stick spoon.

6 When the joint is cooked, wrap with foil, keep warm and allow to rest for 5–10 minutes.

HOW DO YOU LIKE YOUR MEAT COOKED?

Rare – drops of blood are visible on the surface when cut. The meat is spongy to the touch. Ideal for beef, game, kidneys and lamb.

Medium – meat should be pink in colour with some pink juices in the centre. Meat will resist when pressed. Ideal for beef, lamb, kidneys and liver.

Well done – meat should be one colour all through, firm to the touch and the juices should run clear. It is essential that pork and poultry are cooked right through.

Roast beef with Yorkshire pudding

1 × 1kg (2lb) joint lean beef
   (topside)
1 onion, finely diced
1 carrot, diced
1 celery stick, diced
2 tsps mixed dried herbs
1 tbsp soy sauce diluted in 2
   tbsps water (optional)
1 tbsp gravy powder

for the Yorkshire pudding batter
115g (4oz) plain flour
1 egg
pinch of salt
150ml (¼ pint) skimmed milk

1 Preheat the oven to 190C, 375F, Gas Mark 5.

2 Prepare the beef by removing as much fat as possible. Weigh the joint and calculate the cooking time.

3 Place the onion, carrot, celery and herbs in the bottom of a roasting tin or ovenproof dish, and pour 300ml (½ pint) of water over to keep moist.

4 Place a wire rack inside the tin and sit the beef on top.

5 Season well. Using a pastry brush, baste the joint with the diluted soy sauce and cover with aluminium foil. Place in the oven.

6 Halfway through the cooking time, baste again to prevent the meat from drying out.

7 Forty minutes before the beef is ready, make the Yorkshire pudding batter by blending the flour with the egg and a little milk to a smooth paste. Add the salt and whisk in the remaining milk until smooth.

8 Preheat a 6-hole, non-stick Yorkshire pudding tin for 2 minutes in the oven. Remove and half-fill each mould with batter. Increase the oven temperature to 200C, 400F, Gas Mark 6, place the pudding batter in the oven and cook for 35–40 minutes.

9 When the beef is cooked, remove it from the roasting tin and wrap in foil to keep warm. Allow it to rest for 5–10 minutes.

10 Meanwhile, drain the meat and vegetable juices from the roasting tin through a sieve into a fat separating jug. Pour away any fat, then pour the juices into a saucepan. Add 300ml (½ pint) water and heat. Slake the gravy powder with a little water and add to the pan, stirring continuously until the gravy thickens.

11 To serve, carve the beef thinly. Serve with the Yorkshire puddings, fat-free roast potatoes and parsnips (see page 265), low-fat gravy and additional seasonal vegetables.

BEEF GRAVY

1 Drain the juices from the roasting tin through a sieve into a saucepan.

2 Top up with 300ml (½ pint) water, bring to the boil, thicken with gravy powder mixed to a paste with 1–2 tbsps of water, stirring continuously.

SPOT THE DIFFERENCE: YORKSHIRE PUDDING

Left: low fat **79 kcal/1.3g fat**   Right: high fat **148 kcal/7.5g fat**

LOW-FAT GRAVY

Having removed the fat before cooking, there will be very little fat in the beef juices. But for other meats such as lamb and pork and for poultry the roast juices need to have the fat separated after cooking.

1 Drain the meat juices into a gravy separator. The fat will rise to the top.

2 Drain off the meat juices from the bottom of the gravy separator or, if using the bowl method, spoon off the fat from the top. Proceed as for beef gravy from Step 2 opposite.

Pork fillet with sage and apricots

Adding herbs to this simple pork dish transforms it into something special. The meat can be prepared in advance and stored in the refrigerator until ready to cook. If you wish, you can roast the pork in the oven without the sauce and serve the sauce separately.

Serves 4
1 serving 480 kcal/12g fat
Preparation time 20 minutes
Cooking time 50 minutes

115g (4oz) ready to eat dried
    apricots
4 pork fillets (approx. 175g/6oz
    each in weight)
8 sage leaves
8 thin slices Parma ham
2 red onions, finely chopped
2 garlic cloves, crushed
2 small celery sticks, sliced
300ml (½ pint) vegetable stock
1 tbsp plain flour
2 tsps chopped fresh lemon
    thyme
1 cinnamon stick
2–3 pieces lemon peel
600ml (1 pint) tomato passata
½ wineglass dry white wine
2 tbsps chopped fresh flat leaf
    parsley
salt and freshly ground black
    pepper

1 Preheat the oven to 200C, 400F, Gas Mark 6.

2 Place the apricots in a bowl and cover with boiling water to soften.

3 Remove any fat from the pork fillets. Using a sharp knife, create a pocket in each fillet by slicing down the centre to open out the meat.

4 Drain the apricots and push into the centre of the fillets with the sage leaves.

Roll the fillets back into shape and wrap 2 slices of Parma ham around each piece.

5 Preheat a non-stick frying pan or wok. Season the pork with salt and black pepper. Pan-fry the pork over a high heat to seal the meat, then place in an ovenproof dish.

6 Add the onions, garlic and celery to the pan or wok and soften. Add 2–3 tbsps of stock, then sprinkle the flour over. Mix well, 'cooking out' the flour for 1 minute.

7 Gradually stir in the remaining stock and add the remaining ingredients except the parsley. Bring the sauce to the boil to allow it to thicken, then pour it over the pork. Cover with foil and place in the centre of the oven for 30–35 minutes.

8 Remove from the oven and, just before serving, stir in the parsley.

Garlic and rosemary-spiked lamb with blueberry glaze

This sweet and succulent lamb dish is full of flavour. If you cannot find blueberries, dark plums cut in quarters make a good alternative.

Serves 4
1 serving 449 kcal/18g fat
Preparation time 15 minutes
Cooking time 2–2½ hours

1 × 1kg (2lb) leg of lamb, skin
    removed
2 garlic cloves, sliced
3–4 sprigs fresh rosemary
300ml (½ pint) meat stock
2 tbsps tomato purée
lemon zest
225g (8oz) fresh blueberries
salt and freshly ground black
    pepper

1 Preheat the oven to 180C, 350F, Gas Mark 4.

2 Using a small sharp knife, make incisions all over the lamb. Push slices of garlic and small sprigs of rosemary into the holes and season with salt and pepper.

3 Place the lamb on a wire rack over a roasting tin. Pour 1 pint of water into the tin to prevent the fat burning in the base of the tin. Cover with foil and place in the oven for 1–1½ hours.

SECRETS OF SUCCESSFUL CARVING

1 Place the meat on a flat surface. Always make sure your carving knife is sharp, and use a carving fork to hold the meat securely.

2 Always carve with the blade of the knife facing away from you, using long cutting strokes the full length of the knife.

3 Meat should be carved across the grain, as this leads to more tender slices.

4 Beef should be thinly sliced, and lamb fairly thick.

Topside of beef – slice thinly across the grain.

Leg of lamb – hold the bone firm with kitchen paper or a cloth. Slice at an angle on both sides of the bone.

4 Place the stock, tomato purée, lemon zest and blueberries in a small saucepan and bring to the boil. Simmer until the sauce thickens.

5 When the lamb is cooked, remove from the rack and place on a serving dish. Brush the lamb with the blueberry sauce.

6 Serve with seasonal fresh vegetables.

Rack of lamb with garlic herb crust

Rack of lamb is delicious but does have quite a thick layer of fat on top. This sweet herby crust keeps the meat moist and adds lots of flavour.

Serves 4

1 serving 378 kcal/ 18g fat

Preparation time 20 minutes

Cooking time 30 minutes

1 × 8-rib rack of lamb

1 tbsp redcurrant jelly

2 smoked garlic cloves, crushed

25g (1oz) fresh white breadcrumbs

2 tsps chopped fresh rosemary

2 tsps chopped fresh thyme

2 tsps chopped fresh mint

salt and freshly ground black pepper

1 Preheat the oven to 190C, 375F, Gas Mark 5.

2 Using a sharp knife, remove the fat from the outside of the lamb.

3 In a small bowl mix together the redcurrant jelly and garlic until smooth. Spread the mixture over the lamb.

4 Mix together the breadcrumbs and herbs in a shallow dish. Season with salt and black pepper. Carefully dip the lamb into the breadcrumbs, pressing down well to make the crumbs stick to the lamb.

5 Place the lamb in a roasting tray and press any remaining crumbs onto the surface of the lamb. Roast in the centre of the oven for 25 minutes.

6 Remove from the oven and allow to stand for 5 minutes. Slice the lamb in between the bones and allow 2 cutlets per person. Serve hot with additional redcurrant jelly.

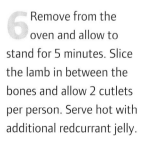

Poultry

Chicken is rich in protein and low in fat, but chicken skin is a no-no on a low-fat diet. So why pay for something that's not required? Buy skinless chicken – minced, cubed or as whole breasts.

Poultry farming has expanded in recent years and now offers carefully produced free range and organically fed birds with a fuller flavour than factory farmed birds. Turkey meat is also very lean, and makes a good alternative to chicken.

It is essential to store chicken properly chilled and also to make sure the poultry is completely cooked. Always test before serving and never serve poultry undercooked.

How to joint a whole chicken

CUTTING INTO EIGHT PIECES

1 Place the whole chicken on a chopping board. Using a sharp chopping knife, split the skin where the leg joins the carcass.

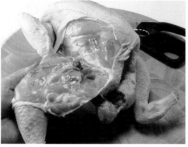

2 Pull one leg away from the carcass, twisting to break the joint. Carefully cut away the meat, keeping the knife as close to the carcass as possible. Repeat to remove the other leg.

3 Pull the skin tight and cut the leg joint in half across the natural line on the skin.

4 Remove the wing tips from both wings.

5 Make an incision between one wing and the breast and cut right through the joint. Repeat with the other wing.

6 Using heavy duty scissors, cut away the breast plate from the remaining carcass.

7 Cut the breast in half.

8 Remove the skin from all the pieces by pulling away with the aid of a chopping knife.

Stir-fries

Stir-frying is probably the quickest and easiest form of cooking. You can cook strips of meat alongside fresh vegetables and a selection of seasonings and create a simple, tasty meal in minutes. Careful preparation will add style and sophistication to any stir-fry.

Quick and easy chicken

Serves 2
1 serving 270 kcal/3g fat
Preparation time 5 minutes
Cooking time 30 minutes

2 × 115g (2 × 4oz) boneless
   chicken breasts, skin removed
1 can or jar any low-fat cooking
   sauce (max. 5% fat)
freshly ground black pepper

1 Preheat a non-stick frying pan or wok.

2 Cut each chicken breast into thin strips.

3 Add the chicken breasts to the pan or wok, add plenty of black pepper, and cook over a high heat, moving the chicken around the pan to ensure an even heat distribution.

4 When the chicken is almost cooked, pour in the cooking sauce and stir well. Reduce the heat and simmer for 5 minutes to ensure the chicken is completely cooked through to the centre.

5 Serve with boiled rice.

Stir-fried chicken with ginger and orange

Serves 4
1 serving 260 kcal/3.1g fat
Preparation time 25 minutes
Marinating time 1 hour
Cooking time 15 minutes

4 medium skinless chicken breasts
2 tbsps dry sherry
zest and juice of 2 oranges
2 tbsps runny honey
2 tbsps plum sauce
1 small Thai chilli, finely sliced
2 garlic cloves, crushed
1 × 2.5cm (1in) piece ginger, peeled and finely chopped
1 tbsp tomato purée
½ tsp five spice powder
1 red pepper, finely sliced
2 small courgettes, finely sliced
50g (2oz) pak choi or dark cabbage
salt and freshly ground black pepper
orange slices to garnish

1 Prepare the chicken by removing all traces of fat, then cut the chicken into long thin strips and place in a shallow dish.

2 Combine the sherry, orange juice and zest, honey and plum sauce. Mix well and add the chilli, garlic, ginger, tomato purée and spice powder.

3 Pour the mixture over the chicken, cover and place in the refrigerator for 1 hour to marinate.

4 Preheat a non-stick wok or large frying pan. To test the pan is hot enough, add 1 piece of raw chicken. If it sizzles, the pan is at the right temperature. Lift the chicken pieces from the marinade, add to the hot pan, and cook over a high heat for 5–6 minutes, turning the pieces regularly.

5 Wash the pak choi well and place in a colander to drain. Slice or chop the vegetables.

6 When the chicken has completely changed colour and is firm to the touch, add the prepared vegetables, tossing all the ingredients together. Season to taste. Add the remaining marinade and allow to heat through.

7 Transfer to a hot serving dish, and garnish with orange slices.

CHICKEN – WHY REMOVE THE SKIN?

The skin on poultry and meat is where most of the fat is found. By buying skinless chicken or removing the skin before cooking, you automatically cut down the fat content of the recipe.

Nutritional values based on 115g (4oz)

Chicken breast with skin	**173 kcal**	**6.4g fat**
Skinless chicken breast	**148 kcal**	**2.2g fat**

Spicy lemon chicken

A great family chicken dish. Lemongrass is available fresh or dried, but using fresh lemongrass will enhance the finished dish.

Serves 4
1 serving 146 kcal/2.5g fat
Preparation time 10 minutes
Marinating time 1 hour
Cooking time 15 minutes

**450g (1lb) skinless chicken
    breast
zest and juice of 1 lemon
2 tbsps light soy sauce
1 tsp ground coriander
150ml (¼ pint) tomato passata
1 small red chilli, finely sliced
1 tsp finely chopped lemongrass
2 garlic cloves, crushed
salt and freshly ground black
    pepper
1 tbsp chopped fresh coriander**

1 Using a sharp knife, cut the chicken breast into dice and place in a shallow dish. Season with salt and black pepper. Combine the remaining ingredients, except the fresh coriander, and pour over the chicken. Leave to marinate for at least 1 hour, mixing occasionally.

2 Strain away the marinade from the chicken and reserve. Preheat a non-stick wok or frying pan and dry-fry the chicken quickly over a high heat for 5–6 minutes, turning it to seal all sides

3 Add the reserved marinade and continue to cook for a further 10 minutes, to allow the sauce to simmer gently and thicken. Stir in the fresh coriander and serve.

Turkey and pepper stroganoff

Serves 4
1 serving 280 kcal/3.4g fat
Preparation time 30 minutes
Cooking time 15 minutes

450g (1lb) lean cooked turkey
    flesh, cut into strips
1 medium onion, chopped
1 red pepper, seeded and diced
2 garlic cloves, crushed
300ml (½ pint) chicken stock
1 tbsp plain flour
150ml (¼ pint) Madeira wine
225g (8oz) small chestnut
    mushrooms, sliced
2 tsps Dijon mustard
300ml (½ pint) virtually fat free
    fromage frais
2 tbsps chopped fresh parsley
salt and freshly ground black
    pepper
pinch of paprika to dust
4 lemon wedges to garnish

1 Preheat a non-stick frying pan or wok. Spray with a little olive oil spray to coat the pan and add the cooked turkey and the onion. Dry-fry for 2–3 minutes until the onion starts to soften.

2 Add the red pepper and garlic and cook for a further minute.

3 Add 2–3 tbsps of the stock and sprinkle the flour over. Mix well with a wooden spoon and 'cook out' the flour for 1 minute.

4 Add the remaining stock and the Madeira wine, stirring continuously. Add the mushrooms, stir in the mustard and cook for a further 2–3 minutes.

5 Remove the pan from the heat and stir in the fromage frais and parsley.

6 Check the seasoning, dust with paprika and garnish with lemon wedges.

Pheasant wrapped in Parma ham with red wine

Pheasant has a much stronger flavour than most poultry, although the breast meat has a much lighter flavour than that of the dark leg meat.

Serves 4
1 serving 350 kcal/15g fat
Preparation time 20 minutes
Cooking time 40 minutes

4 pheasant breasts (approx. 115g/4oz each), skin removed
4 lean slices Parma ham
1 medium red onion, finely chopped
2 celery sticks, finely chopped
1 chicken stock cube dissolved in 300ml (½ pint) water
1 tbsp plain flour
225g (8oz) chestnut mushrooms, sliced
1 wineglass red wine
2 tbsps chopped fresh mixed herbs

1 Season the pheasant breasts on both sides with plenty of black pepper, then wrap each breast with a slice of Parma ham. Preheat a non-stick pan. Add the pheasant and dry-fry on both sides for 5–6 minutes until lightly browned. Remove from the pan and place on a plate.

2 Add the onion to the pan and cook gently until lightly coloured.

3 Add the celery and 2 tbsps of stock. Sprinkle the flour over and 'cook out' for 1 minute.

4 Gradually stir in the remaining stock with the mushrooms and wine.

5 Return the pheasant to the pan and add the herbs. Simmer gently for 15–20 minutes until the sauce has reduced and the pheasant is cooked through. Serve with seasonal vegetables.

Casseroles and curries

Casseroles and curries are a favourite family standby. Recreating classic curries and authentic holiday dishes is something we all try from time to time. These easy recipes offer a detailed guide on how to achieve the maximum flavour to impress your family.

Chicken casserole with peppers

This recipe works equally well with lean pork steaks or even turkey breast fillets. The white wine may be substituted with cider or apple juice.

Serves 4
Per serving 304 kcal/4.7g fat
Preparation time 20 minutes
Cooking time 45 minutes

1 medium onion, finely chopped
1 chicken, jointed with skin
    removed
2 garlic cloves, crushed
150ml (¼ pint) chicken stock
2 tbsps plain flour
3 tbsps dry white wine
1 × 400g can chopped tomatoes
1 tbsp chopped fresh tarragon
1 red pepper, diced
1 yellow pepper, diced
salt and freshly ground black
    pepper
1 tbsp chopped fresh parsley

1 Preheat a non-stick pan. Add the onion and dry-fry until soft.

2 Season the chicken on both sides and add to the pan, lightly browning on each side.

3 Remove the chicken and keep warm.

4 Add the garlic and 2 tbsps of stock to the onion.

5 Stir in the flour and 'cook out' for 1 minute.

6 Add the remaining stock and the wine and tomatoes.

7 Stir in the tarragon and peppers and bring to the boil.

8 Return the chicken to the pan and cover with a lid. Simmer gently for 30–35 minutes. Before serving, sprinkle with parsley. Serve with seasonal vegetables.

Chicken winter casserole

Serves 4
1 serving 235 kcal/8.6g fat
Preparation time 20 minutes
Cooking time 45 minutes

1 medium onion, finely chopped
4 large skinless chicken breasts
2 garlic cloves, crushed
150ml (¼ pint) chicken stock
1 tbsp plain flour
3 tbsps red wine
1 × 400g can chopped tomatoes
1 tbsp chopped fresh mixed
   herbs
115g (4oz) button mushrooms
115g (4oz) swede, peeled and
   diced
salt and freshly ground black
   pepper
1 tbsp chopped fresh parsley

This all-in-one casserole combines chicken and vegetables in a rich tomato sauce. Fresh herbs give the sauce a real taste of Provence.

1 Preheat the oven to 190C, 375F, Gas Mark 5.

2 Dry-fry the onion in a non-stick frying pan until soft.

3 Season the chicken on both sides and add to the pan, lightly browning on each side.

4 Remove the chicken and place in an ovenproof dish.

5 Add the garlic and 2 tbsps of stock to the onion and stir in the flour. 'Cook out' for 1 minute, then add the remaining stock, wine and tomatoes. Stir in the mixed herbs, mushrooms and swede, and bring to the boil. Pour over the chicken and cover with aluminium foil.

6 Place in the centre of the oven for 30–35 minutes. Just before serving, sprinkle with chopped fresh parsley.

Lemon-baked guinea fowl

Guinea fowl is a light-flavoured game bird, not as strong in flavour
as pheasant but stronger than chicken.

Serves 4
1 serving 278 kcal/4.2g fat
Preparation time 15 minutes
Cooking time 35 minutes

3 baby leeks, finely chopped
4 skinless guinea fowl breasts
300ml (½ pint) skimmed milk
2 tsps vegetable bouillon stock
  powder
150ml (¼ pint) dry white wine
1 tbsp cornflour
zest and juice of 1 lemon
salt and freshly ground black
  pepper
1 tbsp chopped fresh parsley

1 Preheat the oven to 180C,
350F, Gas Mark 4.

2 Preheat a non-stick pan, add
the leeks and dry-fry until soft.
Place in the bottom of an ovenproof
dish.

3 Season the guinea fowl breasts
on both sides with salt and
black pepper and add to the pan,
browning them on both sides.
Transfer to the ovenproof dish and
place on top of the leeks.

4 Meanwhile, heat the milk, stock
powder and wine in a saucepan.
Slake the cornflour with a little cold
milk and stir into the hot milk.
Reduce the heat and simmer for 2–3
minutes as the sauce thickens,
adding the lemon zest and juice.
Pour the sauce over the guinea fowl
and cover with kitchen foil.

5 Bake in the oven for 20 minutes
until fully cooked through.

6 Transfer to a serving dish and
sprinkle with chopped parsley.
Serve with a selection of green
vegetables and potatoes.

PERFECT CURRIES

Supermarkets sell a wide variety of readymade curry sauces such as korma, balti or madras, but they can sometimes all taste very similar. Nothing compares to a freshly made sauce packed with individual spices and fresh ingredients. Simple cooking techniques can make all the difference.

Onions – virtually all curries start with fried onions. Dry-fry over a moderate heat until they start to colour. The longer you cook them, the more roasted onion flavour will be added to the finished sauce.

Garlic – smoked or roasted garlic will again add extra flavour. To roast garlic simply wrap the whole bulb in a piece of kitchen foil and bake in a hot oven for 20 minutes. Smoked garlic is sold in some supermarkets as loose bulbs or in strings just like regular garlic.

Spices – always use fresh spices where possible. Once opened they soon lose their flavours. Some spices such as fresh chillies and lemongrass can be frozen for use at a later date.

Tomatoes – use good quality fresh or canned tomatoes. If using fresh, you can add tomato wedges directly to a curry. However, skinning them and remove the seeds will give a smoother finish to the sauce. Fresh tomatoes skin very easily by dropping into boiling water for 10 seconds. Cut in half and remove the seeds with a teaspoon.

Coconut and coriander chicken

This mild creamy chicken dish is truly delicious served with rice or noodles. Chopping the coriander really fine turns the colour of the sauce a soothing pale green.

Serves 4
1 serving 282 kcal/4.3g fat
Preparation time 15 minutes
Cooking time 30 minutes

4 skinless chicken breasts, cut into chunks
2 medium red onions, finely chopped
2 garlic cloves, crushed
2 tsps ground coriander
150ml (¼ pint) hot vegetable stock
1 tbsp plain flour
1 × 400ml can reduced-fat coconut milk
1 tbsp chopped fresh coriander
2 tbsps virtually fat-free fromage frais
salt and freshly ground black pepper

1 Preheat a non-stick pan or wok. Season the chicken pieces with salt and pepper and dry-fry in the pan or wok for 6–7 minutes until they start to colour. Remove from the pan and set aside.

2 Add the onions and garlic to the pan or wok and cook gently until soft.

3 Add 2 tbsps of stock and mix well. Add the ground coriander and the flour and 'cook out' for 1 minute.

4 Gradually add the remaining stock and the coconut milk, stirring continuously to prevent any lumps from forming.

5 Return the chicken to the pan or wok and simmer gently for 10 minutes to ensure the chicken is fully cooked.

6 Remove from the heat, stir in the chopped coriander and the fromage frais. Serve immediately.

Green Thai chicken curry

Marinating the chicken overnight maximises the flavour of this very spicy curry. Once cooked, the finished curry can be stored chilled of frozen and reheated as required. For a milder curry, substitute green peppers for the green chillies.

Serves 4
1 serving 305 kcal/4.7g fat
Preparation time 25 minutes
Marinating time 1 hour
Cooking time 30 minutes

for the curry paste
3 garlic cloves, peeled
1 tbsp ground coriander
½ tsp ground turmeric
¼ tsp fenugreek seeds or
   ground fenugreek
2–3 small whole fresh green
   chillies
seeds removed from 8 crushed
   cardamom pods
2 tsps chopped fresh lemongrass
2 tsps vegetable stock powder

4 large skinless chicken breasts,
   cut into pieces
1 large red onion, finely chopped
1 tbsp tamarind paste or hot
   fruit chutney
4 kaffir lime leaves
1 × 400ml can reduced-fat
   coconut milk
1 tbsp cornflour
2 tbsps chopped fresh coriander

1 Make the paste by grinding all the ingredients in either a food processor or liquidiser. Scrape the paste into a bowl, then rinse out the food processor bowl with a little water.

2 Add the chicken pieces to the paste and mix well. Allow to marinate for a minimum of 1 hour or ideally overnight.

3 In a non-stick pan dry-fry the onion until soft, then add the chicken and cook for 5–6 minutes, stirring continuously. Add the remaining ingredients except the cornflour and fresh coriander.

4 Slake the cornflour with a little cold water and stir into the sauce. Simmer gently for 15–20 minutes until the sauce thickens and the chicken is cooked through. Just before serving, stir in the fresh coriander.

Tunisian chicken

Orange juice forms part of this rich spicy sauce.
Vegetarians can substitute Quorn or soya for the chicken.

Serves 4
1 serving 280 kcal/3.8g fat
Preparation time 10 minutes
Cooking time 40 minutes

1 large red onion, finely sliced
4 skinless chicken breasts, cut
   into strips
2 garlic cloves, chopped
1 tsp coriander seed
1 tsp ground cumin
1 tsp ground cinnamon
½ tsp cayenne pepper
6 cardamom pods, crushed with
   seeds removed
300ml (½ pint) chicken stock
2 tbsps plain flour
1 tbsp chopped fresh oregano
1 × 400g can chopped tomatoes
2 pieces orange peel
150ml (¼ pint) orange juice
salt and freshly ground black
   pepper

1 Preheat a non-stick frying pan. Dry-fry the onion for 2–3 minutes until soft. Add the chicken and garlic and cook briskly, turning the chicken regularly to seal on all sides.

2 Add the spices with 2–3 tbsps of stock and sprinkle the flour over. Mix well, 'cooking out' the flour for 1 minute.

3 Gradually mix in the remaining stock. Add the oregano, tomatoes, orange peel and juice. Cover and simmer gently for 20 minutes.

4 Season to taste and serve hot with couscous or rice.

Chicken jalfrezi

You can substitute diced beef or lamb for the chicken. Just allow 20 minutes' extra cooking time to allow the meat to tenderise. For vegetarians Quorn fillets work really well.

Serves 4
1 serving 288 kcal/5g fat
Preparation time 10 minutes
Cooking time 25 minutes

4 skinless chicken breasts
1 tsp ground cumin
1 tsp ground coriander
2 tsps garam masala
1 × 2.5cm (1in) piece fresh ginger, finely chopped
2 red onions, diced
1 red and 1 green pepper, seeded and diced
2 garlic cloves, crushed
1 small red chilli, sliced
juice of 1 lime
2 tsps vegetable bouillon stock powder
900g (2lb) tomato passata
1 tbsp chopped fresh coriander
salt and freshly ground black pepper
1 tbsp chopped fresh mint to garnish

1 Slice the chicken into bite-sized pieces, season with a little salt and black pepper and place in a bowl. Add the cumin, ground coriander, garam masala and ginger and mix well.

2 Preheat a non-stick wok until hot. Dry-fry the onions, peppers and garlic for 2–3 minutes until they start to colour.

3 Add the chicken and continue cooking for 5–6 minutes as the chicken starts to change colour. Add the remaining ingredients except the fresh coriander and mint. Reduce the heat and simmer gently for 20 minutes.

4 Just before serving stir in the coriander and mint. Spoon into a warmed serving dish and garnish with mint leaves.

Oven-baked chicken tikka masala

Oven-baked means no additional fat is required. The yogurt adds a rich smooth creamy texture as well as toning down the spicy flavour.

Serves 4
1 serving 334 kcal/9.6g fat
Preparation time 10 minutes
Cooking time 25 minutes

4 skinless, boned chicken
   breasts
600ml (1 pint) tomato passata
300ml (½ pint) low-fat natural
   yogurt
2 tbsps chopped fresh coriander
salt and freshly ground black
   pepper
mint leaves to garnish

for the tikka paste
1 small red onion
4 tbsps tomato purée
1 tsp ground cumin
½ tsp ground cinnamon
1 × 2.5cm (1in) piece fresh
   ginger, grated
2 garlic cloves, crushed
1 small red chilli, seeded and
   chopped
juice of 1 lime
2 tsps vegetable bouillon stock
   powder

1 Preheat the oven to 200C, 400F, Gas Mark 6. Cut the chicken into chunks, place in a bowl and season well with salt and black pepper.

2 Place the tikka paste ingredients in a food processor and blend until smooth. Spread the tikka mixture over the chicken, coating on all sides. Leave to marinate for 20 minutes.

3 Transfer to a non-stick roasting tin and place in the oven for 15 minutes until lightly roasted. Remove from the oven and stir in the tomato passata.

4 Return to the oven for a further 10 minutes to heat through. Just before serving, stir in the yogurt and coriander. Spoon into a warmed serving dish and garnish with mint leaves.

Roasting

Simple roast chicken can be enjoyed by everyone – just remember to remove the skin before serving. Breast meat is much leaner than the leg or thigh, as the fat drips down through the bird as it cooks.

Try to drain away as much fat from the cooking juices when making the accompanying gravy.

Lemon roast chicken with fresh herb stuffing

Serves 4
1 serving 425 kcal/13g fat
Preparation time 30 minutes
Cooking time 1–1½ hours

**1 medium free range or organic
   chicken (approx. 1.5kg/3lb)
1 medium onion, finely chopped
2 garlic cloves, crushed
115g (4oz) fresh breadcrumbs
1 tbsp each chopped fresh
   thyme and parsley
2 tsps chopped fresh rosemary
2 lemons
300ml (½ pint) hot chicken stock
600ml (1 pint) chicken stock
1 tbsp gravy powder**

1 Preheat the oven to 180C, 350F, Gas Mark 4.

2 Prepare the chicken by washing well inside and out. Remove as much skin as possible from the surface of the chicken and season with salt and freshly ground black pepper.

3 Make the stuffing by dry-frying the onion and garlic in a preheated non-stick pan for 4–5 minutes until soft. Add the breadcrumbs and herbs with a little black pepper.

4 Mix in the stock and 1 tsp of lemon zest, then remove from the heat and allow to cool.

5 Once cool, spoon the stuffing into the neck cavity, the smaller of the 2 cavities, and press in well. Press the remaining stuffing onto the chicken, covering the outside. Push one lemon inside the other cavity. Squeeze the juice from the remaining lemon and pour over the chicken.

6 Place the chicken on a rack over a non-stick roasting tin, cover with foil and place in the oven for 1–1½ hours, depending on the size of the chicken (allow 30 minutes per 450g/1lb plus an extra 30 minutes).

7 Once cooked, remove the chicken from the roasting tin and wrap with foil to keep hot.

8 Rinse out the tin with 600ml (1 pint) chicken stock and pour through a sieve into a gravy separator. Drain off the juices, and heat in a saucepan. Thicken with gravy powder.

HOW TO CARVE A CHICKEN

First slice down in between the carcass and the leg joint. This will identify if the chicken is completely cooked. The leg should then pull away easily, slicing through the joint.

Carve the breast meat into small, thin slices.

Low-fat duck with black cherries

A delicate fruity sauce rounds off this exotic dish. Duck meat without the fatty skin is very lean.

Serves 4
1 serving 468 kcal/4.7g fat
Preparation time 5 minutes
Cooking time 20 minutes

4 × 175g (4 × 6oz) duck breasts
1 × 270g jar morello cherries
few sprigs fresh thyme
150ml (¼ pint) orange juice
2 tsps arrowroot
chopped fresh mint leaves
salt and freshly ground black
**   pepper**

1 Preheat the oven to 200C, 400F, Gas Mark 6.

2 Prepare the duck by removing all the skin with a sharp knife. Season each breast well with salt and pepper. Using a sharp knife, slash the duck several times and place in an ovenproof dish.

3 Heat the cherries, thyme and orange juice in a saucepan. Mix the arrowroot with a little cold water to a paste and stir into the sauce. Simmer until thickened, then pour the sauce over the duck.

4 Place in the oven for 10–12 minutes.

5 Remove the duck from the oven and allow to rest for 5 minutes.

6 Strain the juices from the roasting dish into the sauce and stir in the chopped mint. Carve the duck into pieces and serve with the hot cherry sauce and green vegetables.

Fish and shellfish

With the wide variety of fish available, it makes sense to include more fish in our weekly menu planning. Fresh fish is probably the easiest option on a low-fat diet. High in protein and naturally low in fat, it takes only minutes to cook. When choosing fresh fish, check that it is firm, brightly coloured and wet in appearance. Oily fish, such as salmon and mackerel, contain essential fatty acids that are important for good health, and so can be eaten in moderation on a low-fat eating plan.

There are many ways of cooking fish – dry-frying, steaming/poaching, and grilling or baking in foil or paper. Dry-frying is suitable for lightly breaded fillets of flat fish or goujons (thin strips), and strips or fillets of plaice, lemon sole and salmon. Thick cuts of fish such as cod and haddock are ideal for poaching or steaming as they tend to retain their shape and texture as well as keeping moist. Fish steaks such as salmon, cod and tuna can be placed on a lightly greased baking tray and grilled lightly on each side, and non-stick griddle pans are perfect for cooking firm, meaty fish steaks such as fresh tuna or swordfish.

Crispy golden plaice with spinach sauce

Fine polenta flour or cornmeal makes an interesting coating for fish, meats and some vegetables.
It absorbs moisture from the food as it cooks, resulting in a crisp golden coating.

Serves 4
1 serving 404 kcal/6.7g fat
Preparation time 15 minutes
Cooking time 20 minutes

4 × ½ fillets fresh plaice, skinned
1 egg, beaten
8 tbsps fine polenta flour or
    cornmeal
a little vegetable oil
3 baby leeks, finely chopped
150ml (¼ pint) dry white wine
300ml (½ pint) skimmed milk
2 tsps vegetable bouillon stock
    powder
1 tbsp cornflour
2 handfuls fresh spinach, finely
    shredded
salt and freshly ground black
    pepper
whole tomatoes and lemon
    wedges to garnish

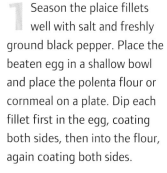

1 Season the plaice fillets well with salt and freshly ground black pepper. Place the beaten egg in a shallow bowl and place the polenta flour or cornmeal on a plate. Dip each fillet first in the egg, coating both sides, then into the flour, again coating both sides.

2 Preheat the oven to 180C, 350F, Gas Mark 4. Preheat a non-stick frying pan. Spray the pan lightly with cooking spray oil. Alternatively, add a little vegetable oil to the pan, then wipe out, using a wad of absorbent kitchen paper.

3 When the pan is hot, add sufficient fillets of fish to cover the base of the pan. Cook for 2–3 minutes, then flip the fillets over and cook for a further 2–3 minutes. Transfer the fish to a baking tray and place in the oven to keep warm.

4 In a separate non-stick pan dry-fry the leeks until soft. Add the wine, milk and stock powder to the saucepan and heat gently. Slake the cornflour with a little cold milk and stir into the hot milk. Reduce the heat and simmer for 2–3 minutes as the sauce thickens. Add the spinach and season to taste.

5 Transfer the fish to a serving dish and garnish with tomatoes and lemon wedges.

Creamy grilled lobster

Cooked lobsters are available in some supermarkets.
You can ask for the lobster to be split in order to save preparation time.

Serves 1
1 serving 228 kcal/3.4g fat
Preparation time 10 minutes
Cooking time 15 minutes

**1 cooked lobster (approx.
500g/1¼lb)**
¼ tsp English mustard powder
¼ tsp cayenne pepper
1 tbsp chopped fresh chives
**150ml (¼ pint) low-fat natural
yogurt**
**25g (1oz) low-fat mature
Cheddar cheese, grated**
**salt and freshly ground black
pepper**

1 Using a sharp knife, split the lobster in half lengthways by placing the point of the knife into the centre and pressing down through the shell. Remove the dark vein-like canal which runs along the length of the tail. Take out the meat from the main shell and place on a chopping board. Remove the stomach, which is under the head, and throw away. Throw away also the spongy material between the shell and the meat.

2 Chop the lobster meat and place in a small mixing bowl. You can add the liver (a soft creamy mass) to the meat.

3 Add the mustard, cayenne pepper, chives and yogurt. Season well with salt and black pepper and mix the ingredients together. Carefully spoon the meat mixture back into the lobster shell and sprinkle with the cheese.

4 Place under a hot grill until golden brown and piping hot.

5 Just before serving, crack the claws, using lobster crackers or a rolling pin, to make it easier to remove the claw meat.

6 Serve hot with salad or a selection of vegetables.

Spicy prawn masala

A delicious creamy curry with lots of unusual flavours. For a vegetarian option, replace the prawns with Quorn pieces or a selection of root vegetables.

Serves 4
1 serving 146 kcal/
   1.5g fat
Preparation time 25
   minutes
Cooking time 20 minutes

for the paste
3 garlic cloves, peeled
3 tsps ground coriander
½ tsp ground turmeric
½ tsp ground fenugreek
2–3 small whole fresh
   chillies
seeds removed from 4
   crushed cardamom pods

1 large red onion, finely
   chopped
2 tbsps tomato purée
600ml (1 pint) fish or
   vegetable stock
1 tbsp tamarind paste
4 kaffir lime leaves
450g (1lb) uncooked
   peeled prawns
2 tbsps chopped fresh
   coriander
a little virtually fat-free
   fromage frais

1 Make the paste by grinding all the ingredients in a food processor or liquidiser. Scrape the paste into a bowl, then rinse out with a little stock.

2 In a non-stick pan dry-fry the onion until soft. Add the paste and cook for 2 minutes, stirring continuously.

3 Add the remaining ingredients, except the coriander and fromage frais, and simmer gently for 15–20 minutes until the sauce thickens and the prawns are cooked through.

4 Just before serving, remove from the heat and stir in the coriander and fromage frais.

Arrabbiata prawns

These hot and spicy prawns make a great baked potato topping.

Serves 4
1 serving 87 kcal/0.7g fat
Preparation time 20 minutes
Cooking time 30 minutes

225g (8oz) uncooked peeled prawns
1 red onion, finely chopped
2 garlic cloves, crushed
1 red pepper, seeded and finely diced
1 × 400g can chopped tomatoes
1 red chilli, seeded and finely chopped
8–10 basil leaves
salt and freshly ground black pepper

1 Rinse the prawns well under cold, running water.

2 Preheat a non-stick frying pan. Add the onion and dry-fry for 2–3 minutes until soft.

3 Add the garlic and red pepper and cook for a further 2–3 minutes.

4 Add the prawns and cook for 5-6 minutes.

5 Add the tomatoes and chilli, bringing the sauce to a gentle simmer. The prawns should be firm and cooked through.

6 Season to taste with salt and black pepper. Add the basil leaves and serve with boiled rice.

Griddled swordfish with horseradish cream

Swordfish and tuna steaks are now readily available in most supermarkets. Serve with some simple tasty vegetables and you have the perfect quick meal.

Serves 4
1 serving 246 kcal/8g fat
Preparation time 10 minutes
Cooking time 10 minutes

4 fresh swordfish steaks
225g (8oz) fresh fine green
  beans, cut in half
1 × 115g (4oz) pack cooked
  beetroot
1 small red onion, finely sliced
2 tbsps low-fat fromage frais
2 tsps horseradish sauce
1 tbsp finely chopped fresh
  chives
salt and freshly ground black
  pepper

1 Season the steaks with salt and black pepper and set aside.

2 Cook the green beans in a pan of lightly salted water until tender. Drain, rinse with cold water and place in a bowl.

3 Chop the beetroot into small wedges and add to the beans along with the red onion.

4 Preheat a non-stick griddle pan until hot. Add the steaks and cook for 2–3 minutes on both sides. Remove from the pan, place on a chopping board and allow to rest for 2 minutes.

5 Mix together the fromage frais, horseradish and chives and season well with salt and black pepper.

6 Divide the bean salad between 4 bowls, place a swordfish steak on top of each and top with the horseradish cream.

Baked sea bass with dill and lemon sauce

Sea bass is a firm, meaty fish with large white flakes. It takes very little cooking and can easily dry out, so be cautious not to overcook.

Serves 4
1 serving 210 kcal/4.8g fat
Preparation time 20 minutes
Cooking time 15 minutes

4 whole sea bass, gutted
300ml (½ pint) apple juice
juice of 1 lemon
2 tsps Dijon mustard
2 tsps finely chopped dill
½ tsp ground fennel seed
1 tsp green peppercorns in brine
2 tsps arrowroot
2 tbsps low-fat fromage frais
1 tbsp chopped fresh mint
salt and freshly ground black
  pepper

1 Preheat the oven to 200C, 400F, Gas Mark 6. Place the sea bass on a chopping board and score several times with a sharp knife. Season the fish well on both sides and place on a non-stick baking tray. Place in the centre of the oven for 10–15 minutes.

2 Place the remaining ingredients, except the fromage frais and mint, in a small saucepan over a medium heat, stirring continuously to combine. Bring the sauce to a low simmer.

3 Mix the arrowroot with a little cold water and whisk into the sauce.

4 Just before serving, remove the sauce from the heat and stir in the fromage frais and mint. Arrange the fish in a serving dish and pour the sauce over. Serve with fresh vegetables.

Lemon-baked salmon fillets

Coating delicate flakes of salmon with a lemon-flavoured glaze is an ideal light way of serving fish.
This dish needs to be made in advance to allow the glaze to set before serving.

Serves 6
1 serving 329 kcal/19g fat
Preparation time
   30 minutes
Cooking time 25 minutes
Cooling time 4 hours

6 × 175g (6 x 6oz) salmon
   fillets (or steaks)
2 lemons, sliced
6 sprigs fresh rosemary
sea salt
black pepper
zest of 2 lemons to
   garnish

for the glaze
juice of 1 lemon
150ml (¼ pint) dry white
   wine
2 leaves of gelatine
¼ tsp vegetable bouillon
   stock powder
freshly ground black
   pepper

1 Preheat the oven to 180C,
350F, Gas Mark 4.

2 Wash the salmon fillets well.
Cut 6 pieces of greaseproof
paper large enough to
accommodate each fillet in a
wrapped parcel. Place 1 fillet on a
piece of paper, season the inside
with salt and pepper and place 2
slices of lemon with a sprig of
rosemary on top.

3 Season the top of the fillet and
fold the edges of the paper
over to form a parcel, twisting the
paper to prevent it from unfolding.
Repeat with all 6 fillets. Place in an
ovenproof dish and bake in the oven
for 15–20 minutes, depending on
the thickness of the fillets, then
remove from the oven and allow to
cool.

4 Once cool, unwrap each parcel
and remove the lemon slices
and rosemary. Turn each fillet over
and remove the skin. Transfer to a
plate or tray and refrigerate for at
least 4 hours or overnight.

5 Make the glaze by gently
heating all the ingredients in a
small saucepan until the gelatine has
dissolved. Using a pastry brush,
paint the glaze onto the salmon
fillets and top with the lemon zest.
Return the fillets to the refrigerator
until ready to serve. Garnish with
salad leaves before serving.

Baked salmon with sweet ginger

Sweet and sour flavours enhance this quick and easy fish dish. The fish can also be cooked under a hot grill for 6–8 minutes, depending on the thickness of the fish. Check the fish is cooked by carefully pulling the flesh apart, using 2 knives. The flesh inside should be light pink in colour and not wet in appearance. When cooked, the flesh will flake away from the skin easily.

Serves 4
1 serving 173 kcal/10g fat
Preparation time 20 minutes
Cooking time 10 minutes

2 tbsps lemon juice
4 tsps light muscovado sugar
1 tsp finely chopped fresh
    ginger
4 tsps chopped fresh dill
4 tsps light soy sauce
4 salmon steaks
salt and freshly ground black
    pepper

1 Preheat the oven to 200C, 400F, Gas Mark 6.

2 In a mixing bowl, combine the lemon juice, sugar, ginger, dill and soy sauce to form a glaze, and season with salt and black pepper.

3 Place 1 salmon steak in the bowl and toss in the glaze. Repeat with the remaining 3 steaks. Transfer the salmon to an ovenproof dish and pour the marinade over.

4 Bake in the oven for 8–10 minutes until just cooked. Serve with salad or seasonal vegetables.

Baked smoked haddock with spinach, tomato and ginger

The simple and versatile tomato sauce used here is very low in fat.
It is ideal for coating oven-baked fish or to use as a topping sauce for pasta.

Serves 4
1 serving 191 kcal/2g fat
Preparation time 25 minutes
Cooking times 35 minutes

3 baby leeks, finely chopped
150ml (¼ pint) dry white wine
2 × 400g cans chopped tomatoes
1 × 2.5cm (1in) piece ginger,
    finely chopped
2 tsps vegetable bouillon stock
    powder
250g (8oz) fresh spinach
4 smoked haddock fillets

1 Preheat the oven to 180C,
350F, Gas Mark 4.

2 Preheat a non-stick pan. Add the leeks and dry-fry until soft. Add the
wine, tomatoes, ginger and stock powder and simmer gently for 15
minutes until the sauce has reduced.

3 Chop the spinach and place in the bottom of an ovenproof dish.
Season the fish on both sides with black pepper and place on top
of the spinach.

4 Pour the sauce over the fish and cover with a piece of greaseproof
paper.

5 Bake in the oven for 6–8 minutes until firm
but not overcooked.

Smoked haddock and potato pie

Try to buy naturally smoked fish, which is pale yellow in colour. The bright yellow fish often sold in supermarkets has been dipped into a coloured chemical flavoured dye to give a smoked flavour.

Serves 6
1 serving 268 kcal/1.8g fat
Preparation time 10 minutes
Cooking time 50 minutes

2 baby leeks, finely chopped
2 garlic cloves, crushed
2 tsps finely chopped fresh
   thyme
450ml (¾ pint) skimmed milk
2 tbsps plain flour
150ml (¼ pint) white wine
2-3 tsps mild course grain
   mustard
1½ tbsps chopped fresh parsley
700g (1¾lb) potatoes, peeled
2 tbsps virtually fat-free
   fromage frais
700g (1¾lb) naturally smoked
   haddock
salt and freshly ground black
   pepper
zest of 1 lemon to garnish

1 Preheat the oven to 200C, 400F, Gas Mark 6.

2 Preheat a non-stick saucepan. Add the leeks, garlic and thyme, stirring well. Reduce the heat and add 3 tbsps of milk. Sprinkle the flour over, then stir it in quickly to form a roux. Cook for 1 minute to allow the flour to 'cook out', then gradually mix in the remaining milk.

3 Add the wine, mustard and parsley (reserve a little parsley for the garnish), bringing the sauce to a gentle simmer. Simmer for 10 minutes, stirring occasionally.

4 Meanwhile, boil the potatoes in a saucepan of salted water until well cooked. Drain and mash well until smooth, adding the fromage frais and seasoning well with a little salt and plenty of black pepper.

5 Skin the fish by pulling the skin from the thickest part in the direction towards the tail – it should come away quite easily.

6 Cut the fish into chunks, checking it for bones, and place in the bottom of an ovenproof dish. Cover with the sauce.

7 Using a fork, smooth the potatoes on top. Bake in the oven for 30-40 minutes until golden.

8 Just before serving, garnish with the lemon zest and a little chopped parsley.

Gingered salmon and herb en croûte

This makes an excellent centrepiece to a buffet table.
When cold, it will slice easily into neat portions for serving.

Serves 4
1 serving 530 kcal/26g fat
Preparation time 20 minutes
Cooking time 45 minutes

1kg (2lb) fresh salmon fillet
1 × 2.5cm (1in) piece fresh
   ginger, finely chopped
1 tsp finely chopped fresh lemon
   thyme
1 tbsp chopped fresh parsley
1 tbsp chopped fresh chives
6 spring onions, finely chopped
6 sheets filo pastry
1 egg, beaten with 2 tbsps milk
salt and freshly ground black
   pepper

1 Preheat the oven to 200C, 400F, Gas Mark 6.

2 Prepare the salmon by removing the skin from the bottom of the fish. Season well on both sides with salt and black pepper.

3 Lightly grease a rectangular baking tray slightly longer in length than the salmon. Take 1 sheet of filo pastry and brush with egg. Place the sheet across the end of the baking tray so that it overhangs both sides of the tray. Repeat with 3 more sheets, placing them further along the baking tray.

4 Place the salmon onto the pastry and cover with the ginger and herbs.

5 Fold the pastry over to encase the fish and brush with the egg. Using scissors, cut the remaining pastry into triangles and arrange across the fish, again brushing with egg.

6 Bake in the oven for 20 minutes until golden brown. Serve hot or cold with accompanying salads.

Steamed cod with minted vegetables

Adding mint together with lime zest and juice to the vegetables adds lots of zingy flavour to this recipe.

Serves 2
1 serving 191 kcal/1.7g fat
Preparation time 15 minutes
Cooking time 25 minutes

450g (1lb) thick cod fillet,
    skinned and cut into 2 steaks
1 small red onion, finely sliced
1 garlic clove, crushed
1 small courgette, cut into sticks
1 small red pepper, seeded and
    thinly sliced
1 tbsp chopped fresh mint
juice and zest of 1 lime
salt and freshly ground black
    pepper

1 Remove any bones from the fish and season with salt and black pepper on both sides.

2 Preheat a non-stick pan, add the onion and dry-fry until soft. Add the garlic, courgette and red pepper and cook briskly for 2–3 minutes. Add the mint and the lime and zest and juice and season with salt and back pepper. Remove from the heat.

3 Spoon 2 equal amounts of the vegetables into a steamer basket and place the cod steaks on top. Cover with the remaining vegetables.

4 Cover with a lid and steam over boiling water or in a steamer for 8–10 minutes or until just cooked.

Vegetarian

Many people now choose to include vegetarian meals in their weekly menu plans. For a well-balanced diet, though, it's important to incorporate foods from each of the four main food groups – proteins, milk and dairy products, cereals and grains, and fruit and vegetables.

If you avoid meat or fish completely, you will need to find alternative sources of protein in the form of beans and pulses. Plant-based products include textured vegetable protein (TVP), tofu, which is made from soya beans, and Quorn, a protein based on mushrooms. Low in fat, they are good at absorbing flavours and provide texture and bulk in casseroles, curries and stir-fries.

When choosing dairy products, you can substitute cow's milk with soya milk and other vegetarian alternatives. Look out, too, for reduced-fat vegetarian cheeses, particularly the mature type, which have a strong flavour.

Vegetables cook well in their natural juices and are ideal for dry-frying or stir-frying and roasting. You can add moisture in the form of well-flavoured herb stocks and tomato products such as passata or canned tomatoes, and you can use fruit juices, soy sauce or diluted stock in place of oily marinades.

Spicy chickpea casserole

Serves 4
1 serving 160 kcal/3.8g fat
Preparation time 25 minutes
Cooking time 40 minutes

2 medium leeks, finely chopped
2 courgettes, diced
3 celery sticks, chopped
½ tsp ground cumin
½ tsp ground turmeric
½ tsp ground five spice
2 garlic cloves, chopped
2 tsps chopped fresh oregano
1 × 400g can chickpeas
600ml (1 pint) vegetable stock
2 tsps cornflour
salt and freshly ground black
    pepper
2 pieces fresh orange peel,
    finely shredded
courgette strips to garnish

1 Place the prepared leeks, courgettes and celery and into a preheated non-stick pan and dry-fry for 2–3 minutes until lightly coloured.

2 Add the spices, garlic and oregano and continue to cook for 1 minute.

3 Rinse the chickpeas under cold running water, and add to the pan.

4 Add the stock and bring the mixture to a gentle simmer.

5 Mix the cornflour in a small bowl with a little cold water to a smooth paste.

6 Stir the slaked cornflour into the casserole and simmer gently for 5 minutes.

7 Garnish with the finely shredded orange peel and some finely shredded courgette strips.

Cauliflower and broccoli cheese bake

Cauliflower cheese is a great all-in-one meal. Try this low-fat version which includes a little Parmesan cheese in the topping. Simply delicious!

Serves 4
1 serving 177 kcal/5.2g fat
Preparation time 15 minutes
Cooking time 35 minutes

450g (1lb) cauliflower cut in florets
450g (1lb) broccoli
300ml (½ pint) skimmed milk
1 tbsp vegetable stock powder or 1 vegetable stock cube
4 tsps cornflour
1 tbsp mild Dijon mustard
50g (2oz) low-fat Cheddar, grated
1 tbsp chopped fresh chives
salt and freshly ground black pepper
2 tsps grated Parmesan cheese

1 Preheat the oven to 190C, 375F, Gas Mark 5.

2 Cook the cauliflower and broccoli separately in boiling salted water until tender, drain through a colander and place in the bottom of an ovenproof dish.

3 In a saucepan, heat the milk with the stock. Dissolve the cornflour in a little cold water and stir into the sauce. Stir continuously as the sauce thickens, then reduce the heat and simmer for 2–3 minutes.

4 Stir in the remaining ingredients, except the Parmesan cheese, and season with salt and black pepper.

5 Pour the sauce over the vegetables and sprinkle with the Parmesan cheese. Bake in the oven for 20 minutes until golden brown.

Marjoram stuffed peppers

These peppers can be made in advance and reheated as required. Red and yellow peppers tend to taste sweeter than green, but if you like the flavour use all three.

Serves 4
1 serving 201 kcal/5.6g fat
Preparation time 10 minutes
Cooking time 40 minutes

115g (4oz) fresh white breadcrumbs
1 tbsp chopped fresh marjoram
4 red and 4 yellow peppers
4 shallots, finely chopped
2 garlic cloves, crushed
1 × 400g can artichoke hearts, drained and chopped
salt and freshly ground black pepper

1 Preheat the oven to 200C, 400F, Gas Mark 6.

2 Scatter the breadcrumbs over the base of a non-stick baking tin. Add the marjoram and season well with salt and black pepper. Bake in the oven for 20 minutes, turning every so often to prevent the edges from burning.

3 Slice the tops off the peppers, scoop out and discard the inner seeds. Remove the stalk from the tops and chop the tops very finely.

4 Preheat a non-stick frying pan. Add the shallots and garlic and dry-fry until soft. Add the chopped pepper tops and continue to cook for 4–5 minutes. Add the artichoke hearts and toasted breadcrumbs. Mix together all the ingredients and season to taste.

5 Spoon the filling into the pepper shells, and place them side by side in an ovenproof dish. Cover with foil and bake in the centre of the oven for 20 minutes.

6 Remove the foil and return to the oven for a further 5 minutes to brown.

7 Serve with hot new potatoes and either a large mixed salad or vegetables.

Asparagus vegetable bake

Serves 4
1 serving 466 kcal/10g fat
Preparation time 15 minutes
Cooking time 35 minutes

225g (8oz) baby carrots,
  chopped
225g (8oz) baby parsnips,
  chopped
1 vegetable stock cube
115g (4oz) baby leeks, chopped
115g (4oz) broccoli florets
2 large courgettes, sliced
large bunch baby asparagus
600ml (1 pint) skimmed milk
1 tbsp grain mustard
1 tbsp cornflour
115g (4oz) low-fat Cheddar
  cheese
2 tbsps chopped fresh chives

Packs of small baby vegetables are readily available. As they are mostly pre-trimmed they can be cooked straight from the pack.

1. Preheat the oven to 190C, 375F, Gas Mark 5.

2. Place the carrots, parsnips and stock cube in a small saucepan. Cover with water and boil for 4 minutes. Add the leeks, broccoli, courgettes and asparagus and continue to cook for 2–3 minutes until the broccoli is just cooked.

3. Remove from the heat, drain through a colander and place in the bottom of an ovenproof dish.

4. Add the milk and the mustard to the pan and heat. Slake the cornflour with a little cold water and mix into the milk. Bring to the boil, stirring continuously. Remove from the heat and stir in the cheese and chives.

5. Pour the sauce over the vegetables and place in the oven for 20 minutes until golden brown.

6. Serve with a mixed salad and crusty bread.

GETTING THE MOST FROM ASPARAGUS

English asparagus has a short season, so it's best to make the most of it while it's around. A few basic steps can improve your enjoyment of this delicious vegetable.

- Asparagus should be pre-graded into the same thickness sized pieces to ensure even cooking.

- Thin stalks (sprue) are ideal for soups and sauces as they cook very quickly.

- Medium to thick stalks should be peeled. Using a vegetable peeler, peel away a thin strip 5cm (2in) from the base of each stem. This will take away the skin from the toughest part of the stalk and make the whole stem tender to eat.

- Extra thick stalks are great cooked on a barbecue or griddle. After peeling, blanch in boiling water and place directly on the hot grids.

Tallegio cheese and mushroom stuffed red onions

Tallegio is an Italian creamy, soft cheese with a strong flavour. It is lower in fat than Cheddar cheese and, used in small quantities, adds a good flavour.

Serves 4
1 serving 166 kcal/4g fat
Preparation time 10 minutes
Cooking time 35 minutes

8 medium red onions

2 garlic cloves, finely chopped

115g (4oz) chestnut mushrooms, finely chopped

50g (2oz) Tallegio cheese, cut into small dice

2 tbsps good quality balsamic vinegar

4 ripe tomatoes, skinned, seeded and diced

1 tbsp chopped fresh parsley

salt and freshly ground black pepper

1 Preheat the oven to 200C, 400F, Gas Mark 6. Preheat a non-stick pan.

2 Peel the onions and, using a chopping knife, trim off the top and bottom. Make a large cross on the top side of each onion, cutting halfway down the onion. Cut another cross to give 8 sections per onion. Using an apple corer, carefully remove the centres from each onion and finely chop. Place the chopped onion in the preheated, non-stick pan with the garlic and the mushrooms. Dry-fry for 5–6 minutes until the mixture has cooked down.

3 Add half of the Tallegio cheese and season with salt and black pepper, then mix in the balsamic vinegar and tomatoes.

4 Place the onion shells in an ovenproof dish and fill with the mushroom mixture.

5 Cook in the oven for 30–35 minutes until soft.

6 Five minutes before serving, top with the remaining cheese.

Wild mushroom stroganoff

When selecting fresh mushrooms, always choose dry, firm ones with a light appearance, not dark and wet, as these will add a grey black tinge to the sauce. Dried wild mushrooms make a good substitute, but they need to be soaked in boiling water for 2–3 hours before using – 75g (3oz) dried mushrooms will reconstitute to 450g (1lb) as required in this recipe.

Serves 4
1 serving 80 kcal/1.3g fat
Preparation time 10 minutes
Cooking time 10 minutes

2–3 shallots, finely chopped
2 garlic cloves, crushed
150ml (¼ pint) vegetable stock
1 tbsp plain flour
450g (1lb) mixed fresh wild mushrooms (e.g. oyster, ceps, and shitake)
2–3 sprigs fresh lemon or common thyme
1 wineglass white wine
2 tsps mild Dijon mustard
300ml (½ pint) low-fat Normandy fromage frais
2 tbsps chopped fresh flat leaf parsley
salt and freshly ground black pepper
paprika to garnish

1. Preheat a non-stick frying pan. Add the shallots and garlic and dry-fry until soft. Add 2–3 tbsps of stock to the pan and sprinkle the flour over. Stir well, 'cooking out' the flour for 1 minute.

2. Add the mushrooms and thyme, seasoning well with salt and plenty of freshly ground black pepper. Gradually stir in the remaining stock and white wine. Add the Dijon mustard and simmer gently for 2–3 minutes to allow the sauce to thicken.

3. Remove the pan from the heat and stir in the fromage frais and parsley. Check the seasoning and serve dusted with a little paprika.

Cornmeal pizza margherita

This giant-sized pizza offers a really good portion. If you wish, you can divide the dough into individual pizzas and freeze complete with the topping.

Serves 4
1 serving 297 kcal/4.7g fat
Preparation time 10 minutes
Cooking time 35 minutes

for the dough
175g (6oz) strong white bread flour
50g (2oz) fine cornmeal or polenta flour
1 tsp salt
15g (½oz) fresh yeast or 2 tsps dried yeast
150ml (¼ pint) warm skimmed milk

for the topping
300ml (½ pint) tomato passata
8 cherry plum tomatoes, cut in half
50g (2oz) low-fat Cheddar cheese, grated
60g (2¼oz) half-fat mozzarella cheese
a few basil leaves

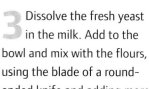
1 Preheat the oven to 200C, 400F, Gas Mark 6.

2 Place the white bread flour and cornmeal or polenta flour in a large mixing bowl. Add the salt and make a slight well in the centre.

3 Dissolve the fresh yeast in the milk. Add to the bowl and mix with the flours, using the blade of a round-ended knife and adding more liquid if required. Turn out onto a floured surface and knead well to form a soft dough. Cover with a damp cloth for 10 minutes.

4 Knead the dough again. Roll it out into a large circle and place on a non-stick baking tray or pizza pan.

5 Spoon the passata onto the base, leaving a border around the edge. Scatter the cherry tomatoes on top and cover with the grated Cheddar and the mozzarella cheese.

6 Bake near the top of the oven for 20 minutes. Just before serving, scatter with basil leaves. Serve hot.

Roasted butternut squash and tomato tart

Serves 6
1 serving 185 kcal/5.9g fat
Preparation time 40 minutes
Cooking time 20 minutes

1 medium butternut squash
2 garlic cloves, sliced
1 tbsp light soy sauce
6 sheets filo pastry
    (30cm × 20cm/12in × 8in)
1 egg white, beaten
1 tbsp fresh thyme leaves
2 tsps vegetable bouillon stock
    powder
115g (4oz) low-fat Cheddar
    cheese
2 eggs, beaten
8 cherry tomatoes
1 tbsp chopped fresh chives
salt and freshly ground black
    pepper

Butternut squash has a smooth velvety texture. Serve this low-fat tart hot with vegetables or cold with salad.

1 Preheat the oven to 190C, 375F, Gas Mark 5.

2 Peel, seed and roughly dice the squash and place in the base of a baking tray. Cover with the garlic and drizzle with soy sauce. Bake in the top of the oven for 20 minutes or until soft.

3 Lightly grease a 23cm (9in) flan tin. Unfold the filo pastry. Taking one sheet at a time, lightly brush with egg white and place in the base of the tin. Continue placing the other sheets on top, tucking the edges into the sides of the tin and brushing each sheet with egg white.

4 Bake in the oven for 4–5 minutes until dry. Allow to cool.

FILO PASTRY

Filo pastry is a boon when it comes to low-fat pastry. Most traditional pastry recipes contain at least 50 per cent fat in the form of butter or margarine. Filo pastry, however, is made in a different way, similar to that of a pasta dough, using just a little vegetable oil with water and lengthy kneading to develop the gluten in the flour. This allows the dough to be rolled extremely thin.

Filo pastry is difficult to make at home and the ability to roll out the dough to such a thin sheet requires great skill. Fortunately, it is readily available, usually frozen. Follow these simple steps for a quick and low-fat way to enjoy pastry.

1 Always allow the pastry to defrost fully at room temperature to prevent the sheets from crumbling.

2 Keep the pastry covered with a damp tea towel, as it soon dries out and becomes brittle.

3 Use one sheet at a time, keeping the bulk covered until ready to use.

4 Cut the pastry to the required shape or size before brushing with egg, as once brushed it will become limp and difficult to handle.

5 Instead of melted butter, brush the pastry with egg white or a mixture of whole egg beaten with a little milk.

6 Cook the prepared pastries straight away to prevent sogginess.

5 To make the filling, place the roasted squash and garlic in a mixing bowl. Add the thyme, stock powder, cheese and eggs and mix together, seasoning to taste. Spoon into the pastry case and arrange the tomatoes on top.

6 Bake in the oven for 15–20 minutes until set. Serve warm.

Leek and mushroom tart

Serves 6
1 serving 145 kcal/5.4g fat
Preparation time 40 minutes
Cooking time 30 minutes

**6 sheets filo pastry
(30cm × 20cm/12in × 8in)**
1 egg white, beaten
4 medium leeks, sliced
2 garlic cloves, crushed
**115g (4oz) chestnut mushrooms,
sliced**
2 tsps chopped fresh thyme
2 eggs
1 tbsp chopped fresh parsley
**1 tsp vegetable bouillon stock
powder**
**75g (3oz) mature low-fat
Cheddar cheese**
1 tbsp chopped fresh chives
**salt and freshly ground black
pepper**

This savoury tart is best served cold as you may find it difficult
to cut when hot.

1 Preheat the oven to 190C,
375F, Gas Mark 5. Lightly
grease a 23cm (9in) flan dish with a
little vegetable oil. Brush one sheet
of filo pastry with egg white and
place in the bottom of the flan dish.
Repeat with the remaining sheets,
placing the sheets at slight angles to
each other and brushing with
beaten egg white in between each
layer.

2 To make the filling, preheat a
non-stick frying pan until hot.
Add the leeks and garlic and dry-fry
for 4–5 minutes until they start to
soften. Add the mushrooms and
thyme and continue to cook for a
further 3 minutes.

3 In a mixing bowl, beat the eggs.
Add the parsley, stock powder
and cheese, reserving 1 tbsp of
cheese for the top. Quickly mix in
the cooked leek mixture and the
chopped chives (reserve some for
the garnish), seasoning with salt and
black pepper.

4 Spoon into the pastry case and
top with the reserved cheese.
Bake in the oven for 20–25 minutes
until set.

5 Remove from the oven and allow to cool for easy slicing.
Garnish with the reserved fresh chives.

Spicy aubergine pastries

These light pastries are delicious served hot or cold. Vary the filling by using other vegetables such as courgettes or peppers.

Serves 4
1 serving 144 kcal/4g fat
Preparation time 20 minutes
Cooking time 60 minutes

1 medium onion, finely diced
2 garlic cloves, crushed
2 aubergines, diced
1 tbsp curry powder
2 tsps vegetable bouillon
  powder
300ml (½ pint) tomato passata
1 egg
3 tbsps skimmed milk
4 sheets filo pastry
1 tsp paprika

1 Preheat the oven to 200C, 400F, Gas Mark 6.

2 Preheat a non-stick frying pan, add the onion and garlic and dry-fry until soft.

3 Add the aubergines and continue cooking over a moderate heat as the aubergine starts to soften. Sprinkle the curry powder over and 'cook out' for 1 minute, stirring well.

4 Add the stock powder and passata. Simmer gently for 15–20 minutes until the liquid has reduced to leave a thick paste. Allow to cool.

5 Beat together the egg and milk. Take one sheet of filo pastry and brush with the egg mixture. Fold the pastry in half to form a smaller rectangle. Brush again with egg, then place a good tbsp of the mixture in a line at one end of the pastry. Fold the end of the pastry over to cover the mixture.

6 Brush again with egg, then fold in the pastry at both sides. Roll the pastry up to form a spring roll shape.

7 Brush with egg and place on a non-stick baking tray. Repeat, using the remaining pastry.

8 Bake in the oven for 20–25 minutes until golden brown.

9 When cooked, slice in half and serve with mixed salad leaves.

Minted sprout and chestnut roast

This delicious vegetarian roast can be served either hot or cold. Cooked in individual ramekins, it also makes a great hot starter.

Serves 4
1 serving 273 kcal/5.3g fat
Preparation time 25 minutes
Cooking time 40 minutes

**2 medium onions, finely
    chopped
2 garlic cloves, crushed
225g (8oz) Brussels sprouts
50g (2oz) prepared chestnuts,
    chopped
1 large red pepper, seeded and
    finely diced
175g (6oz) red lentils
1 × 400g can chopped tomatoes
150ml (¼ pint) vegetable stock
2 tsps chopped fresh thyme
2 eggs, beaten
1 tbsp finely chopped mint
salt and freshly ground black
    pepper
fresh basil to garnish**

1 Preheat the oven to 200C, 400F, Gas Mark 6.

2 Preheat a non-stick frying pan. Add the onions and garlic and dry-fry for 3–4 minutes until soft. Add the sprouts and chestnuts and continue cooking for a further 5 minutes, seasoning well with salt and black pepper. Remove from the stove.

3 In a saucepan bring to the boil the lentils, tomatoes, stock and thyme. Simmer gently for 15 minutes to soften the lentils and allow them to absorb the liquid.

4 Mix together the contents of both pans in a mixing bowl, adding the beaten egg and chopped mint. Pour the mixture into a lightly greased 900g (2lb) loaf tin and stand in a baking tray containing 2.5cm (1in) water.

5 Bake in the middle of the oven for 40 minutes until risen and set. Allow to cool slightly. Just before serving, sprinkle with fresh basil.

Aubergine and coconut milk Thai curry

As with many Thai-style curries, the sauce should be slightly thickened just to add body. Try to hunt out reduced-fat coconut milk, which has all the flavour of the real thing.

Serves 4
1 serving 139 kal/8g fat
Preparation time 20 minutes
Cooking time 20 minutes

1 large aubergine, cut into 2.5cm (1in) cubes
2 small shallots, finely sliced
1 tsp coriander seed
2 smoked garlic cloves, crushed
2 tsps lemongrass, finely chopped
small piece fresh ginger, peeled and finely chopped
1 Thai red chilli, sliced
300ml (½ pint) reduced-fat coconut milk
300ml (½ pint) vegetable stock
1tbsp cornflour
1 tbsp virtually fat-free Normandy fromage frais
4 ripe tomatoes, cut into quarters
1 tbsp chopped fresh coriander leaves

1 Preheat a large non-stick pan or wok. Add the aubergine and shallots and dry-fry for 8–10 minutes until soft.

2 Crush the coriander seed on a chopping board with the broad side of a chopping knife and add to the pan along with the garlic. Cook for 2–3 minutes, then add the lemongrass, ginger and chilli, stirring well to combine the spices. Add the coconut milk and vegetable stock and bring to the boil. Reduce the heat and simmer gently for 5 minutes.

3 Slake the cornflour with a little cold milk and stir into the curry. Continue stirring as the sauce thickens.

4 Just before serving, remove from the heat and stir in the fromage frais, tomato quarters and coriander leaves. Serve with boiled noodles.

Quorn red Thai curry

Quorn is a member of the fungi family and makes a good substitute for chicken and other meats especially in highly flavoured curries. Serve this curry on a bed of basmati rice or noodles.

Serves 4
1 serving 130 kcal/2.4g fat
Preparation time 10 minutes
Cooking time 20 minutes

1 large red onion, finely chopped
2 garlic cloves, crushed
300g (10oz) fresh or frozen
    Quorn pieces
1 tsp ground coriander
1 tsp finely chopped lemongrass
1 red pepper, finely sliced
600ml (1 pint) tomato passata
1 small red chilli, finely sliced
1 Kaffir lime leaf
salt and freshly ground black
    pepper
1 tbsp chopped fresh coriander

1 Preheat a non-stick wok or frying pan. Add the onion and garlic and dry-fry for 2–3 minutes until soft. Add the Quorn pieces and season well with salt and black pepper. Stir in the ground coriander and lemongrass.

2 Add the remaining ingredients and bring to a gentle simmer. Reduce the heat and allow to simmer for 10 minutes until the sauce has reduced slightly.

3 Just before serving add the chopped fresh coriander.

Roast vegetable and lentil dhal

Roasting the vegetables in this simple vegetable curry adds a strong depth of flavours. For a more creamy curry, stir in 2 tbsps of low-fat natural yogurt just before serving.

Serves 4
1 serving 220 kcal/1.8g fat
Preparation time 25 minutes
Cooking time 40 minutes

2 medium onions, finely chopped
2 courgettes, diced
1 small aubergine, diced
1 large red pepper, seeded and diced
175g (6oz) red lentils
1 × 400g can chopped tomatoes
150ml (¼ pint) vegetable stock
2 garlic cloves, crushed
2 tsps chopped fresh thyme
2 tsps garam masala curry powder
8 cardamom pods, crushed and seeds removed
salt and freshly ground black pepper
fresh mint to garnish

1 Preheat the oven to 200C, 400F, Gas Mark 6.

2 Place the prepared vegetables into a roasting tin, season well with salt and black pepper and bake at the top of the oven for 25–30 minutes until lightly roasted.

3 In a large saucepan, bring to the boil the lentils, tomatoes, stock, garlic, thyme and spices.

4 Simmer for 15–20 minutes to soften the lentils and allow them to absorb the liquid.

5 Add the roasted vegetables and simmer for 10 minutes to allow the flavours to combine.

6 Just before serving, sprinkle with fresh mint.

Parsnip and red pepper cakes with red pepper relish

These tasty parsnip cakes can be made in advance and frozen. The relish adds moisture to the finished dish.

Serves 4
1 serving 290 kcal/3.8g fat
Preparation time 20 minutes
Cooking time 30 minutes

1kg (2lb) fresh young parsnips
4 small leeks, sliced
1 red pepper, seeded and diced
1 garlic clove, crushed
2 tsps chopped fresh thyme
2 tbsps virtually fat-free
  fromage frais
1 tbsp finely chopped chives
50g (2oz) fresh breadcrumbs
salt and freshly ground black
  pepper

for the red pepper relish
6 red peppers, halved and
  seeded
1 red onion, finely chopped
1 garlic clove, crushed
2–3 tsps chilli sauce

1 Preheat the oven to 200C, 400F, Gas Mark 6.

2 Top and tail the parsnips. Cut into small pieces and place in a saucepan. Cover with water and boil until soft. Drain well and return to the pan. Mash with a potato masher until smooth, adding plenty of salt and black pepper.

3 Preheat a non-stick pan. Add the leeks and diced pepper and dry-fry until soft. Add the garlic and thyme, mixing well.

4 Combine the parsnip and leek mixtures, and add the fromage frais and chives. Allow to cool.

5 When cool, form the mixture into 8 potato cake shapes and roll in the fresh breadcrumbs.

6 Place the cakes on a baking tray and bake near the top of the oven for 10–15 minutes until golden brown.

7 To make the red pepper relish, place the peppers on a non-stick baking tray and roast in the oven for 30 minutes until they are well charred.

8 Remove the peppers from the oven and place immediately into a plastic food bag. Seal the bag and allow to cool.

9 When cool, remove the peppers and peel away the skins. Chop the flesh into small dice.

10 Dry-fry the onion and garlic for 2 minutes, then add the peppers and chilli sauce. Spoon into a serving bowl.

11 Serve the parsnip and red pepper cakes with the relish.

Spanish omelette

This classic recipe tastes just as good cold as part of a buffet selection. If you wish, you can add a splash of milk to the beaten eggs, although the dry-fried vegetables will produce some liquid.

Serves 4
1 serving 174 kcal/10g fat
Preparation time 10 minutes
Cooking time 10 minutes

1 red onion, finely sliced
1 red pepper, seeded and diced
1 garlic clove, crushed
6 chestnut mushrooms, finely sliced
6 eggs, beaten and seasoned with salt and black pepper
4 tomatoes, skinned, seeded and finely diced
1 tbsp finely chopped flat leaf parsley

1 Preheat a non-stick frying pan. Add the onion, pepper, garlic and mushrooms and dry-fry for 3–4 minutes until soft.

2 Add the beaten egg and cook gently, bringing the set mixture from around the outside of the pan into the centre with a wooden spatula.

3 When the omelette is almost completely set, add the diced tomatoes and parsley and turn the omelette over either whole or split down the centre to make it easier.

4 Cut into small squares and serve hot or cold with salad.

Rice and couscous

There are many different types of rice grains, and they all add variety and texture to a low-fat diet. Basmati, white and brown, is a good source of vitamin B and a great choice for those with a gluten or wheat intolerance. Brown rice also has a medium glycaemic index, which can aid digestion.

Always rinse rice well under cold running water before cooking to remove some of the starches. This will help to keep the rice fluffy and loose once cooked.

At 100 calories per 25 grams, rice is quite high in calories. To help it go further, mix each portion of boiled rice with 2–3 handfuls of beansprouts. These are low in calories and high in flavour and fibre.

If using canned beansprouts, just drain them and add to the boiling rice for about 30 seconds, and drain together. If using fresh beansprouts, place in a bowl, pour boiling water over them and drain along with the rice. Fresh beansprouts contain 31 kcal and 0.5g fat per 100g, and canned beansprouts just 10 kcal and 0.1g fat per 100g.

Rice and couscous

When cooking rice, add a vegetable stock cube to the cooking water instead of salt. This will enhance the flavour without increasing the fat and calorie content.

Couscous is a precooked wheat semolina and a staple food of North Africa where it is traditionally served with a meat or vegetable stew. It is low in fat and contains B vitamins and iron. Cooked couscous can also be combined with onions and other ingredients and served cold as a salad.

COMMON VARIETIES OF RICE

American long-grained This is a good, flavoursome grain and has a long narrow kernel. The grains cook very loosely and remain separated after cooking. Available white or brown.

Basmati Grown in the foothills of the Himalayas, this thin grain has a light aromatic flavour. Shorter than American long grain rice, it becomes fluffy during cooking. It can be soaked in advance to withstand longer cooking. Available white or brown.

Easy cook This is par-cooked and then dried. It cooks much more quickly than any forms of rice and produces loose, separate grains. Available white or brown.

Thai fragrant rice This is a sweet, fragrant rice that becomes slightly sticky during cooking, with the grains tending to clump together. It produces a light fluffy texture. Available white.

Arborio and Carnoroli These Italian short, broad grains are used in risotto dishes because of their ability to absorb liquid, which plumps up the grain. The grains become creamy and slightly sticky during cooking and give a nutty flavour. Available white.

Calasparra Spanish in origin, this is a hardy grain suitable for paellas. The grains remain firm during cooking and produce a slightly sticky texture. Available white.

Wild Not a grain as such but a black grass harvested from the lakeland shores of Minnesota in the United States. It requires cooking for up to 50 minutes and has a nutty, earthy flavour and a chewy texture.

Red Camareine This reddish-brown grain comes from the wetlands of Camareine in France. It takes on a similar appearance to wild rice during cooking and has a woody, nutty flavour and slightly sticky texture.

Pudding rice These short, fat, smooth grains are used in puddings as a thickening agent and produce a creamy smooth texture.

Flaked rice These are shavings of rice, used in puddings. This rice cooks quickly and produces a smooth-like texture.

OTHER RICE PRODUCTS

Sake This is a Japanese rice wine similar to a very dry sherry and is used in savoury dishes.

Mirin Similar to Sake but slightly sweeter, this is used in marinades and dressings.

Rice vinegar Available clear, red, yellow or black, this has a slightly sharp flavour and is used in stir-fries, dressings and marinades.

Rice noodles These white dry threads vary in thickness. They only need to be soaked in boiling water to reconstitute and are used in stir-fries or steamed dishes.

Ground rice This is a gluten-free thickening agent used in puddings and desserts.

Rice flour A very fine flour used for Chinese dim sum dumplings, this is gluten free and can be used as a substitute for wheat flour.

Fragrant rice

Adding just a few spices to rice really makes quite a difference. Kaffir lime leaves add a unique flavour. If you have difficulty in obtaining them, try fresh bay leaves as a substitute.

Serves 4
1 serving 200 kcal/4.9g fat
Preparation time 15 minutes
Cooking time 30 minutes

1 medium onion, finely chopped
1 garlic clove, crushed
1 tsp crushed coriander seed
6 cardamom pods, crushed with
   seeds removed
good pinch of saffron
175g (6oz) basmati rice
450ml (¾ pint) vegetable stock
2 kaffir lime leaves (optional)
good bunch of fresh basil leaves
salt and freshly ground black
   pepper
lemon and lime wedges to
   garnish

1 Preheat a non-stick pan. Add the onion and garlic and dry-fry until soft. Add the coriander seed and cardamom and continue to cook for 3–4 minutes.

2 Add the saffron and rice and stir in the stock. Bring to the boil, and add the kaffir lime leaves. Reduce the heat and cover with a lid. Simmer gently for 20 minutes until all the stock has been absorbed. Add a little more stock if the mixture appears a little dry.

3 Once the rice is fully cooked, add the shredded basil. Just before serving, garnish with wedges of lemon and lime.

Stir-fried vegetable rice

Add a little extra to your rice by mixing the grains with a few vegetables. As well as adding flavour, it lightens the carbohydrate content of the complete dish.

Serves 4
1 serving 154 kcal/1.2g fat
Preparation time 10 minutes
Cooking time 10 minutes

1 large red onion, finely chopped
1 red pepper, finely diced
225g (8oz) cooked basmati rice
115g (4oz) cooked wild rice
6 cardamom pods, crushed and
   seeds removed
zest and juice of 1 lime
pinch of ground cinnamon

1 Preheat a non-stick frying pan or wok. Add the onion and red pepper and dry-fry for a few minutes until soft. Gradually add the remaining ingredients.

2 Toss the pan well to coat the rice grains. Serve hot or cold as a rice salad.

Roasted red onion rice

Roasted onions have a sweet toasted flavour that really makes a difference to cooked rice. Choose a good quality easy cooking rice, as this will contain less starch and make the rice more free flowing.

Serves 6
1 serving 162 kcal/1.4g fat
Preparation time 15 minutes
Cooking time 30 minutes

6 red onions, peeled
1 tsp crushed coriander seed
1 garlic clove, crushed
good pinch of saffron
175g (6oz) basmati rice
450ml (¾ pint) vegetable stock
salt and freshly ground black
    pepper
chopped fresh coriander to
    garnish

1 Preheat the oven to 200C, 400F, Gas Mark 6.

2 Cut the onions in half, then cut each half into small wedges and place in a roasting tray. Sprinkle with the coriander seed and season well with salt and black pepper. Roast in the oven for 15–20 minutes until soft.

3 Remove from the oven and transfer the onions to a large saucepan, add the garlic, saffron and rice and stir in the stock. Bring to the boil. Reduce the heat and cover with a lid.

4 Simmer gently for 20 minutes until all the stock has been absorbed. Add a little more if the mixture appears a little dry. Once the rice is fully cooked, taste, adjusting the seasoning as required, and transfer to a serving dish.

5 Garnish with chopped fresh coriander.

Semi-dried tomato and saffron risotto

Serves 4
1 serving 351 kcal/4.7g fat
Preparation time 10 minutes
Cooking time 35 minutes

1 medium red onion, finely
   chopped
2 garlic cloves, crushed
225g (8oz) Arborio risotto rice
good pinch of saffron
600ml (1 pint) vegetable stock
½ wineglass white wine
225g (8oz) semi-dried or
   sun-dried tomatoes
2 tbsps low-fat fromage frais
salt and freshly ground black
   pepper
3 tbsps Parmesan cheese
finely chopped chives to garnish

Semi-dried tomatoes are similar to sun-dried tomatoes but are not dried out completely. They have a strong concentrated flavour and a soft texture.

1 Preheat a non-stick pan. Add the onion and garlic and dry-fry until soft. Add the rice and saffron and gradually stir in the stock and wine, allowing the rice to absorb it before adding more – this will take between 15 and 20 minutes.

2 Once all the liquid has been added, stir in the tomatoes, cover and reduce the heat to a gentle simmer until all the mixture has been absorbed. Remove from the heat and fold in the fromage frais. Season with salt and black pepper.

3 Serve hot with a little Parmesan cheese and a sprinkling of chopped chives.

Roasted vegetable rice salad with smoked paprika

Roasting the vegetables in the oven adds extra flavour to this tasty rice salad. Keep refrigerated if made in advance and use within three days of making. Smoked paprika adds a slightly spicy edge to the rice.

Serves 6
1 serving 217 kcal/2g fat
Preparation time 20 minutes
Marinating time 30 minutes
Cooking time 1 hour 20 minutes

1 small gourd
1 red pepper and 1 yellow
    pepper, seeded
1 red onion
2 tbsps light soy sauce
juice of 1 lemon
1 garlic clove, crushed
450g (1lb) cooked mixed grain
    rice
1 tsp smoked paprika
1 tbsp chopped fresh coriander
salt and freshly ground black
    pepper

1 Preheat the oven to 200C, 400F, Gas Mark 6.

2 Prepare the vegetables by slicing into wedges about 1cm (½in) thick. Place in a roasting tin and season well with salt and black pepper.

3 Combine the soy sauce, lemon and garlic in a small bowl and drizzle over the vegetables. Allow the vegetables to marinate for 30 minutes.

4 Once marinated, mix the vegetables well and place in the oven to roast for 35–40 minutes until soft with slight charring around the edges.

5 Place the cooked rice in a large bowl and season well with salt and black pepper. Add the smoked paprika along with the cooked vegetables and mix well. Sprinkle with chopped coriander and serve.

Saffron risotto cakes with tarragon cream

Saffron is a magical spice which adds a rich golden colour to rice as well as a unique flavour. These risotto cakes can be made in advance and stored refrigerated for up to 3 days.

Serves 4
1 serving 288 kcal/2.9g fat
Preparation time 10 minutes
Cooking time 30 minutes

1 medium white onion, finely chopped
2 garlic cloves, crushed
225g (8oz) Arborio risotto rice
good pinch of saffron
600ml (1 pint) vegetable stock
½ wineglass white wine
1 tbsp chopped fresh flat leaf parsley
115g (4oz) low-fat fromage frais
2 tbsps chopped fresh tarragon
2 tbsps plain flour
1 tsp vegetable oil
salt and freshly ground black pepper

1 Preheat a non-stick pan. Add the onion and garlic and dry-fry until soft.

2 Add the rice and saffron and gradually stir in the stock and wine, allowing the rice to absorb it before adding more – this will take between 15 and 20 minutes. Once all the liquid has been added and the rice is cooked, remove from the heat and mix in the parsley with 1 tbsp of fromage frais. Season with salt and black pepper and allow to cool.

3 Combine the remaining fromage frais with the tarragon in a small bowl and season with plenty of salt and black pepper. Set aside.

4 Divide the cooled risotto mixture into eight. Place the flour onto a plate and roll the risotto cakes into it, shaping them with a palatte knife.

5 Preheat a non-stick frying pan with the vegetable oil. As soon as the pan is hot, discard the oil and wipe out the pan with kitchen paper.

6 Add the risotto cakes to the pan and cook over a high heat for 4–5 minutes on each side. Keep them warm in a low oven if you need to cook them in batches.

7 Garnish with the tarragon cream and serve hot with an assortment of fresh vegetables.

Chicken couscous salad

An all-in-one meal which is delicious served hot or cold. It is essential to cook the chicken completely before adding the other ingredients, as there is very little cooking time afterwards.

Serves 4
1 serving 326 kcal/4.8g fat
Preparation time 20 minutes
Cooking time 5 minutes

for the dressing
150ml (¼ pint) fresh orange
   juice
2 tsps chopped fresh ginger
1 tbsp good quality white wine
   vinegar
1 tsp Dijon mustard

4 skinless chicken breasts, sliced
   into strips
1 garlic clove, crushed
1 tsp ground coriander
¼ tsp ground turmeric
1 vegetable stock cube,
   dissolved in 400ml (14fl oz)
   boiling water
175g (6oz) couscous
1 tbsp finely chopped chives
1 tbsp chopped fresh basil
4 tomatoes, skinned, seeded and
   diced
½ cucumber, peeled and diced
salt and freshly ground black
   pepper
fresh basil and fresh orange
   wedges to garnish

1 Mix together the dressing ingredients in a large bowl. Add the chicken and toss in the dressing, seasoning well with salt and black pepper.

2 Preheat a non-stick wok or deep non-stick saucepan. Using a slotted spoon, lift the chicken from the dressing, place in the pan and dry-fry for 8–10 minutes until completely sealed and cooked. Add the garlic, coriander and turmeric and continue to cook for 2 minutes.

3 Add the stock and dressing and bring to the boil. Gradually add the couscous, stirring well. Cover with a lid, remove from the heat and allow to stand for 1 minute. Remove the lid and, using 2 forks, fluff up the couscous grains.

4 Add the herbs, tomato and cucumber and mix well, seasoning to taste.

5 Pile into a serving dish and garnish with fresh basil and orange wedges.

5 Pile into a serving dish and garnish with fresh basil and orange wedges.

Chorizo rice

Chorizo is a Spanish salami sausage highly flavoured with spices, particularly paprika. As it is marbled with fat it is essential to dry-fry the chorizo first to release the fat in the same way as minced beef.

Serves 4
1 serving 303 kcal/9g fat
Preparation time 5 minutes
Cooking time 25 minutes

115g (4oz) thinly sliced semi-
    dried chorizo sausage
2 red onions, finely diced
1 garlic clove, crushed
225g (8oz) basmati rice
600ml (1 pint) vegetable stock
2 bay leaves
2 tbsps chopped fresh coriander

1 Preheat a non-stick frying pan. Add the chorizo and dry-fry over a high heat for 2–3 minutes to release the fat. Tip the chorizo into a sieve to drain away the fat. Wipe out the pan, using a good pad of kitchen paper, and return the pan to the heat.

2 Dry-fry the onion and garlic for 1–2 minutes until soft. Add the rice to the pan and return the chorizo. Stir in the stock and add the bay leaf. Bring to the boil, then reduce the heat and simmer gently for 15–20 minutes until the rice is cooked and all the stock has been absorbed.

3 Just before serving, sprinkle with chopped coriander. Serve hot with a side salad or steamed vegetables.

Pasta

There are many different types of pasta available, both fresh and dried. Fresh pasta cooks really quickly and retains more flavour than dried pasta. Shapes and styles of pasta vary from fine noodles to large cannelloni shapes suitable for filling.

Always check the labels carefully when buying fresh or dried pasta as many brands contain high quantities of egg yolk which can increase the calorie and fat content.

Dried pasta should be cooked in a large quantity of boiling water. Adding a vegetable or herb stock cube to the cooking water enhances the flavour and does away with the need to add oil. You can also buy 'no precook' pasta, which is useful for dishes such as lasagne.

Good-quality canned chopped tomatoes and tomato passata with garlic and herbs form a good low-fat base to many tasty pasta sauces and are virtually fat free.

Parmesan cheese is the traditional pasta accompaniment but is very high in fat and calories (4 tsps of grated Parmesan provides 45 kcal and 3.3g fat), so use sparingly.

Beef and mushroom cannelloni

Serves 4
1 serving 490 kcal/18.9g fat
Preparation time 65 minutes
Cooking time 1 hour

450g (1lb) lean minced beef
1 large onion, finely diced
2 garlic cloves, crushed
225g (8oz) chestnut mushrooms,
    finely diced
1 tbsp dark soy sauce
2 beef stock cubes
450g (1lb) tomato passata
1 tbsp chopped fresh oregano or
    marjoram
8 lasagne sheets
salt and freshly ground black
    pepper

for the topping
300ml (½ pint) skimmed milk
1 tbsp vegetable stock powder
    or crumbled stock cube
4 tsps cornflour
1 tsp English mustard powder
1 tbsp white wine
50g (2oz) low-fat mature
    Cheddar cheese
salt and freshly ground black
    pepper

1 Preheat the oven to 200C, 400F, Gas Mark 6.

2 Preheat a non-stick pan, add the beef and dry-fry until cooked. Drain through a sieve to remove the fat. Wipe out the pan, using a wad of kitchen paper.

3 Add the onion and garlic to the pan and cook over a moderate heat for 3-4 minutes until soft. Add the beef, mushrooms and soy sauce, then sprinkle the stock cubes over. Add the passata and herbs and simmer for 15-20 minutes.

4 Meanwhile, cook the lasagne sheets in plenty of salted water until just cooked. Drain and cover with cold water to prevent further cooking. Drain the lasagne again and lay the sheets out flat. Season with salt and pepper.

5 Place 1 sheet in an ovenproof dish and cover the centre (about a third) with the beef mixture. Roll up the sheet into a cylindrical shape and place at one end of the dish. Continue with the remaining sheets and pour any remaining mixture over the top.

6 To make the topping, heat the milk and stock in a non-stick jug or bowl. Add a little cold water to the cornflour to slake it, and stir until dissolved. Stir into the hot milk, stirring continuously until the sauce thickens.

7 Reduce the heat, add the remaining ingredients, season with black pepper and simmer for 2-3 minutes.

8 Pour the sauce over and bake in the oven for 25-30 minutes. Serve hot with salad.

Spinach and ricotta cannelloni

Ricotta cheese is an Italian light curd cheese which is fairly low in fat. Mixing it with low-fat Quark cheese reduces the fat content of the recipe yet still retains a creamy milky flavour.

Serves 4
1 serving 422 kcal/11g fat
Preparation time 10 minutes
Cooking time 40 minutes

225g (8oz) fresh spinach
225g (8oz) ricotta cheese
225g (8oz) Quark (low-fat soft cheese)
2 garlic cloves, crushed
225g (8oz) tomato passata
1 tbsp chopped fresh oregano
16 dried cannelloni tubes
salt and freshly ground black pepper

for the topping
600ml (1 pint) skimmed milk
2 tsps vegetable stock powder
1 tsp English mustard powder
1 tbsp cornflour
1 tbsp white wine
salt and freshly ground black pepper
2 tsps grated fresh Parmesan cheese

1 Preheat the oven to 200C, 400F, Gas Mark 6.

2 Using a large chopping knife, finely chop the spinach and place in a mixing bowl. Add the ricotta, Quark and garlic and mix well, seasoning with lots of salt and freshly ground black pepper.

3 Pour the passata into the bottom of a rectangular ovenproof dish and sprinkle with the chopped oregano.

4 Place the spinach mixture into a piping bag without a nozzle and pipe the filling into the cannelloni tubes. Place the filled pasta on top of the passata.

5 To make the topping, heat the milk, stock powder and mustard in a saucepan to near boiling.

6 Slake the cornflour with the wine and whisk into the hot milk. Season with black pepper and simmer gently to allow the sauce to thicken.

7 Pour the sauce over the pasta and place in the oven for 30 minutes.

8 Serve hot topped with a little Parmesan cheese and a leafy salad.

Fresh salmon pasta salad

A cold pasta salad with flakes of pink salmon. If fresh salmon is unavailable, canned salmon is a good substitute.

Serves 6
1 serving 280 kcal/8.9g fat
Preparation time 10 minutes
Cooking time 25 minutes

2 vegetable bouillon stock cubes
2 × 175g (2 × 6oz) fresh salmon
fillets
225g (8oz) pasta shapes
300ml (½ pint) virtually fat-free
fromage frais
juice of half a lemon
1 small red onion, finely
chopped
1 tbsp chopped fresh chives
pinch of sweet paprika
fresh dill to garnish

1 Crumble 1 stock cube in a saucepan and add a little water. Add the salmon and poach for 8–10 minutes over a low heat. Lift the salmon from the pan and allow to cool.

2 Cook the pasta in a large saucepan of boiling water with the remaining vegetable stock cube. Drain the pasta thoroughly and transfer to a mixing bowl. Add the fromage frais, lemon juice, onion, chives and paprika.

3 Carefully flake the salmon into the bowl, removing any bones and skin. Combine all the ingredients with a large metal spoon, taking care not to over-mix and break up the fish too much. Spoon into a serving dish and chill until required. Garnish with fresh dill.

Smoked haddock pasta

Naturally smoked haddock is much lighter in colour than yellow haddock, which is dipped in a dye to colour the outside of the fish. If unavailable, substitute other smoked fish such as cod or halibut.

Serves 4
1 serving 383 kcal/2.2g fat
Preparation time 10 minutes
Cooking time 40 minutes

225g (8oz) pasta shapes
4 tail fillets naturally smoked
    haddock
300ml (½ pint) skimmed milk
1 red onion, finely chopped
2 garlic cloves, crushed
1 red pepper, seeded and finely
    diced
1 red chilli, seeded and finely
    chopped
3 tsps cornflour
300ml (½ pint) low-fat fromage
    frais
juice of ½ a lemon
8–10 basil leaves
salt and freshly ground black
    pepper

1 Preheat the oven to 180C, 350F, Gas Mark 5.

2 Cook the pasta in boiling salted water. Drain and set aside.

3 Poach the fish in the milk for 10–15 minutes, then allow to cool in the cooking liquor.

4 In a non-stick frying pan dry-fry the onion for 2–3 minutes until soft, add the garlic and red pepper and cook for a further 2–3 minutes. Add the fish cooking liquor and chilli, bringing the sauce to a gentle simmer.

5 Slake the cornflour with a little cold milk, then gradually whisk into the sauce. Season to taste with salt and black pepper.

6 Place the pasta in a mixing bowl and pour the sauce over. Mix in the fromage frais.

7 Carefully flake the fish into the pasta mix, taking care to remove all the skin and bones. Add the lemon juice and basil and mix the ingredients together.

8 Spoon into a serving dish and bake in the oven for 15–20 minutes to heat through.

Springtime noodles

Crisp green vegetables combined with noodles make an ideal healthy light lunch. For a creamy consistency fold in 1–2 tbsps of virtually fat-free fromage frais just before serving.

Serves 4
1 serving 170 kcal/3.7g fat
Preparation time 10 minutes
Cooking time 25 minutes

115g (4oz) fine noodles
2 vegetable stock cubes
1 medium red onion, finely
  chopped
2 garlic cloves, crushed
115g (4oz) baby asparagus
115g (4oz) sugar snap peas
115g (4oz) each fine beans
salt and freshly ground black
  pepper
1 tbsp finely grated Parmesan
  cheese

1 Place the noodles in a large bowl containing the stock cubes and cover with boiling water.

2 In a non-stick wok, dry-fry the onion and garlic until soft. Add the asparagus, peas and beans. Cook quickly over a moderate heat for 8–10 minutes, moving the vegetables around with a spatula. When the vegetables are just cooked, drain the noodles and add to the wok. Season with salt and black pepper.

3 Serve hot with a little Parmesan cheese.

Tomato and lemon penne

Serves 4
1 serving 266 kcal/3.9g fat
Preparation time 20 minutes
Cooking time 30 minutes

225g (8oz) penne pasta
1 red onion, finely chopped
2 garlic cloves, crushed
1 red pepper, seeded and finely
    sliced
1 × 400g can chopped tomatoes
1 red chilli, seeded and finely
    sliced
zest of 1 lemon
8–10 basil leaves, shredded
salt and freshly ground black
    pepper
lemon segments to garnish

Fresh lemon adds a great finishing touch to this simple spicy pasta sauce. To cool it down slightly just before serving, you can stir in a little virtually fat-free fromage frais. This also makes a creamier sauce.

1 Cook the pasta in boiling salted water. Meanwhile, preheat a non-stick frying pan, add the onion and dry-fry for 2–3 minutes until soft. Add the garlic and red pepper and cook for 2–3 minutes more. Add the tomatoes, chilli and lemon zest and bring the sauce to a gentle simmer. Season to taste with salt and black pepper.

2 Drain the pasta and pour into a serving dish.

3 Spoon the sauce over the pasta and sprinkle with the shredded basil leaves. Garnish with the lemon segments and serve with a mixed salad.

Citrus pappardelle stir-fry

Serves 4
1 serving 199 kcal/1.6g fat
Preparation time 10 minutes
Cooking time 20 minutes

175g (6oz) pappardelle or
  ribbon pasta
1 vegetable stock cube
150ml (¼ pint) orange juice
8 spring onions
1 garlic clove, crushed
1 red pepper, seeded and finely
  sliced
115g (4oz) mange tout
1 × 2.5cm (1in) piece fresh
  ginger, peeled and finely
  chopped
2 tsps light soy sauce
juice of 1 lime
salt and freshly ground black
  pepper

Adding pasta to a stir-fry helps to bulk out the ingredients without adding fat. This is an ideal way of using up packet ends of all types of pasta.

1 Cook the pasta in a pan of boiling water containing the vegetable stock cube. Drain, return the pasta to the pan and pour the orange juice over.

2 Heat a non-stick wok or large frying pan. Add the onions and garlic with the pepper and dry-fry for 1–2 minutes.

3 Add the mange tout and ginger and continue to cook over a high heat for a further minute.

4 Pour in the pasta and juice, add the soy and lime juice and toss all the ingredients together. Season with black pepper and a little salt if required.

5 Once the pasta is heated through, transfer to a warmed serving dish and serve immediately.

Tagliatelle with mushroom pesto

A quick and easy low-fat sauce that goes well with many types of pasta. Darker mushrooms will give a much stronger flavour to the finished sauce.

Serves 4
1 serving 236 kcal/2.5g fat
Preparation time 10 minutes
Cooking time 20 minutes

225g (8oz) tagliatelle pasta
1 vegetable stock cube
1 medium onion, finely chopped
2 garlic cloves, crushed
115g (4oz) fresh chestnut
mushrooms
150ml (¼ pint) vegetable stock
1 tbsp chopped fresh mixed
herbs
2 tbsps virtually fat-free
fromage frais
salt and freshly ground black
pepper
1 tbsp fresh Parmesan shavings
a few chopped chives to garnish

1 Cook the tagliatelle in a large pan of boiling water with a stock cube added for extra flavour.

2 Preheat a non-stick pan. Add the onion and garlic and dry-fry until soft. Add the mushrooms, cooking until they soften. Add the stock and stir in the herbs.

3 Pour into a blender or food processor and blend until smooth. Place in a small saucepan and heat gently, seasoning with salt and black pepper.

4 Drain the pasta and pour into a warmed serving dish.

5 Remove the sauce from the heat and stir in the fromage frais. Spoon the sauce on top of the pasta and garnish with Parmesan shavings and chopped chives.

Creamy basil pasta

The low-fat pesto in this recipe is a really tasty light sauce for all types of pasta. It can be made in advance and stored in the refrigerator for up to a week.

Serves 4
1 serving 227 kcal/2.2g fat
Preparation time 20 minutes
Cooking time 15 minutes

225g (8oz) penne pasta
1 vegetable stock cube
2 good bunches fresh basil
1 garlic clove, crushed
2 tbsps virtually fat-free
   fromage frais
1 tbsp grated fresh Parmesan
   cheese
salt and freshly ground black
   pepper

1 Cook the pasta in boiling salted water.

2 Meanwhile, in a small saucepan, dissolve the stock cube in 150ml (¼ pint) of boiling water.

3 Remove the leaves from the basil and place in a food processor or liquidiser with the garlic and hot stock. Blend until smooth to form a pesto.

4 Drain the pasta and return to the hot pan. Add the pesto and fromage frais, mixing well together. Season well with salt and black pepper. Pour into a serving dish and sprinkle with Parmesan cheese.

5 Serve with a mixed salad or fresh spinach.

Vegetables

Fresh vegetables contain little fat and are important for health, so it's good to include a wide variety of different types in your diet. It's so easy to fall into the trap of serving the same plain accompaniments time and time again, so ring the changes and spice up your vegetable selection with a little imagination, taking into account flavours, colours and textures. Adding a few herbs and spices, such as Thai lemongrass or fine balsamic vinegar, can turn a plain vegetable side dish into an aromatic delight.

Although prepared packs of vegetables are a useful standby, they do lose their mineral content and flavour during the packing process. So, where possible, choose fresh, loose, good-quality vegetables for maximum flavour and nutritional value.

It's customary to add a large knob of butter or a drizzle of olive oil as the finishing touch to a dish of vegetables. This unnecessary fat can mask the true flavour of the vegetables. Try, instead, a combination of herbs and spices – even a simple sprinkling of fennel seeds or chopped fresh herbs adds flavour and interest.

Marinated roast vegetables

These marinated roast vegetables are perfect served piping hot from the oven or chilled with salad leaves. Either way, the strong contrasting flavours make this a tasty dish.

Serves 4
1 serving 79 kcal/2.7g fat
Preparation time 10 minutes
Cooking time 40 minutes

2 medium courgettes
1 aubergine
1 red and 1 yellow pepper, seeded
2 baby leeks
1 small bulb of fennel
1 red onion, peeled
4 tbsps lemon juice
2 tbsps light soy sauce
2 tsps lemongrass, finely chopped
2 tbsps chopped fresh marjoram
1 tbsp sesame seeds
salt and freshly ground black pepper
parsley to garnish

1 Preheat the oven to 180C, 350F, Gas Mark 4. Prepare the vegetables by slicing into wedges 5mm (¼in) thick.

2 Combine the lemon juice, soy sauce and herbs in a small bowl.

3 Place the vegetables into a roasting tin, season well with salt and black pepper and spoon the marinade over the vegetables.

4 After 15 minutes, turn the vegetables to ensure even flavouring. Leave for 15 minutes, turn again, and sprinkle with the sesame seeds.

5 Place in the oven and roast for 35–40 minutes until tender and slightly charred around the edges.

6 Sprinkle with parsley and serve hot or allow to cool or serve cold as a salad.

Marinade – the mixture of wine, vinegar, fruit juice, herbs and spices poured over meat, poultry or vegetables before cooking.

Marinate – means to put the food in the marinade, to tenderise it and allow the flavours to penetrate.

Thyme roasted root vegetables

A different way of serving root vegetables. Try to cut them all to the same sized pieces. This will help them to cook evenly.

Serves 4
1 serving 202 kcal/2.5g fat
Preparation time 20 minutes
Cooking time 80 minutes

2 large red onions, cut into wedges
8 carrots, roughly cut
8 parsnips, roughly cut
1 small celeriac, chopped
1 small swede, diced
1 small head celery, sliced
1 bulb fennel, sliced
2 garlic cloves, sliced
2 tbsps light soy sauce
2 tbsps chopped fresh thyme
1 tsp finely chopped lemongrass

1 Preheat the oven to 200C, 400F, Gas Mark 6.

2 After preparing all the vegetables, place in a large non-stick roasting tray, season well with black pepper and mix well. Scatter the garlic slices over and drizzle with soy sauce. Mix again, coating the vegetables with the soy sauce.

3 Place in the top of the oven for 35–40 minutes until soft, turning occasionally.

4 Remove from the oven and add the thyme and lemongrass, mixing all the ingredients together. Return to the oven for a further 10–15 minutes.

Balsamic roasted onions

If you find pickled onions a little sharp, try these sweet crunchy onions as an alternative. They can be served hot or cold.

Serves 4
1 serving 108 kcal/0.4g fat
Preparation time 20 minutes
Cooking time 35 minutes

675g (1½lb) small baby onions, peeled
2 tbsps caster sugar
2 tbsps balsamic vinegar
a few sprigs fresh thyme

1 Preheat the oven to 200C, 400F, Gas Mark 6.

2 Place all the ingredients in a non-stick roasting tray and toss well.

3 Bake in the top of the oven for 30–35 minutes until golden brown.

4 Remove from the oven and place in a serving dish. Serve hot or cold.

Garlic roast peppers

These make great party food. Red and yellow peppers tend to be sweeter than green ones. Serve alongside other stuffed vegetables such as courgettes for a colourful vegetable platter.

Serves 4
1 serving 58 kcal/0.7g fat
Preparation time 20 minutes
Cooking time 35 minutes

2 red and 2 yellow peppers, seeded
12 cherry tomatoes
4 garlic cloves, finely chopped
1 tbsp chopped fresh basil
16 basil leaves
salt and freshly ground black pepper

GARLIC

Nothing beats the full aromatic power of fresh garlic. Adding sliced or chopped garlic at the start of the cooking process gives a gentle flavour. Dry-fry with onions, but be careful not to brown it as this will result in a bitter flavour.

Lightly smoked garlic provides additional flavour as well as taking away the harsh strength. Add to low-fat sauces and dressings.

1 Preheat the oven to 200C, 400F, Gas Mark 6.

2 Cut the peppers into quarters and place in a roasting tray. Cut the tomatoes in half and place a piece inside each pepper quarter. Season well with salt and black pepper. Dot small amounts of the chopped garlic inside the peppers and place in the top of the oven.

3 Roast for 20–25 minutes until they start to soften. Allow to cool.

4 Place a basil leaf in the centre of each pepper quarter.

5 Arrange on a serving plate and sprinkle with chopped garlic. Serve warm or cold.

Stuffed baby vegetables

An interesting and tasty way of serving sweet-tasting baby vegetables.
For a vegetarian option substitute finely chopped chestnut mushrooms for the bacon.

Serves 6
1 serving 39 kcal/1.4g fat
Preparation time 10 minutes
Cooking time 60 minutes

6 baby patty pan gourds
2 baby courgettes
4 rashers lean smoked bacon,
  diced
2 garlic cloves, finely chopped
6–8 large basil leaves
2 tbsps good quality red wine
  vinegar
salt and freshly ground black
  pepper
2 tomatoes skinned, seeded and
  diced
1 tbsp chopped fresh parsley

1 Preheat the oven to 180C, 350F, Gas Mark 4.

2 Slice off the tops of the patty pan and a thin slice from the sides of the courgettes, then scoop out the centres, using a small tsp. Place the vegetable shells in a shallow ovenproof dish and chop the flesh finely.

3 Preheat a non-stick pan. Dry-fry the bacon and garlic for 2–3 minutes. Add the chopped vegetables and continue cooking for 5 minutes.

4 Add the remaining ingredients and remove from the heat.

5 Press the mixture into the vegetable shells. Season the outsides with salt and pepper.

6 Place in the oven and bake for 15–20 minutes or until soft. Serve hot or cold.

Pesto baked tomatoes

Serves 6
1 serving 87 kcal/2.2g fat
Preparation time 10 minutes
Cooking time 10 minutes

6 medium ripe tomatoes

for the pesto
1 vegetable stock cube
2 good bunches fresh basil
1 garlic clove, crushed
1 tbsp peeled cooked chestnuts, finely chopped
2 tsps grated fresh Parmesan cheese
salt and freshly ground black pepper

Basil pesto is traditionally made with olive oil, Parmesan cheese and pine nuts – all high in fat. Try this alternative low-fat version.

1 Preheat the oven to 400F, 200C Gas Mark 6. Cut the tops off the tomatoes and scoop out the insides, using a teaspoon. Dissolve the stock cube in 150ml (¼ pint) boiling water.

2 Pluck the basil leaves from the main plant stem. Reserve 6 leaves for the garnish. Place in a food processor or liquidiser. Add the stock and remaining ingredients and blend until smooth. Season to taste with salt and black pepper and scrape out into a bowl.

3 Fill each tomato with the pesto and place on a non-stick baking tray. Place near the top of the oven and bake for 10–15 minutes until lightly roasted.

4 Remove from the oven and garnish each tomato with a basil leaf. Serve hot or cold.

Soured red cabbage

This flavoursome side dish can be made in advance and reheated in a low oven. It is especially good served cold alongside meats, fish and other buffet foods.

Serves 8
1 serving 86 kcal/0.6g fat
Preparation time 20 minutes
Cooking time 1 hour
   30 minutes

1 medium red cabbage
1 red onion, finely sliced
2 cooking apples, grated
5 juniper berries, crushed
pinch of red chilli flakes
75g (3oz) soft brown sugar
300ml (½ pint) red wine
   vinegar
150ml (¼ pint) vegetable stock
salt and freshly ground black
   pepper
2–3 tbsps virtually fat-free
   fromage frais

1 Preheat the oven to 150C, 300F, Gas Mark 2.

2 Cut the cabbage into quarters lengthways and remove the stalk.

3 Finely shred the cabbage and place in a large mixing bowl. Add the onion, apples, juniper berries and chilli, mixing all the ingredients together thoroughly and seasoning well with salt and black pepper.

4 Pile the mixture into a large ovenproof dish and sprinkle with brown sugar. Pour the vinegar and stock over and cover with greaseproof paper.

5 Bake in the bottom of the oven for 1–1½ hours until soft.

6 Pile into a serving dish and drizzle with the fromage frais. Serve hot or cold as a vegetable accompaniment.

Spiced cauliflower

Browning the onions adds a stronger flavour to this spicy side dish.
If kaffir lime leaves are unavailable, use the zest of a fresh lime instead.

Serves 4
1 serving 64 kcal/1.1g fat
Preparation time 10 minutes
Cooking time 30 minutes

1 medium cauliflower
1 red onion, finely chopped
2 garlic cloves, crushed
½ tsp ground cumin
300ml (½ pint) vegetable stock
1 × 400g can chopped tomatoes
2 kaffir lime leaves
1 tsp cornflour
1 tsp Dijon mustard
salt and freshly ground black
   pepper
2 tbsps chopped fresh parsley

1 Remove the outer leaves from the cauliflower and break the vegetable into florets.

2 Preheat a non-stick pan or wok. Add the onion and dry-fry over a high heat until browned. Add the garlic and cumin, then add the cauliflower florets, the stock, tomatoes and kaffir lime leaves.

3 Bring to the boil, then reduce the heat and simmer gently for 15 minutes until cooked.

4 Slake the cornflour with a little cold water and stir into the cauliflower mixture. Simmer gently for 1–2 minutes, stirring well as the sauce thickens and seasoning with plenty of black pepper.

5 Remove from the heat and stir in the mustard. Sprinkle with parsley and serve.

Vegetables suitable for dry-frying

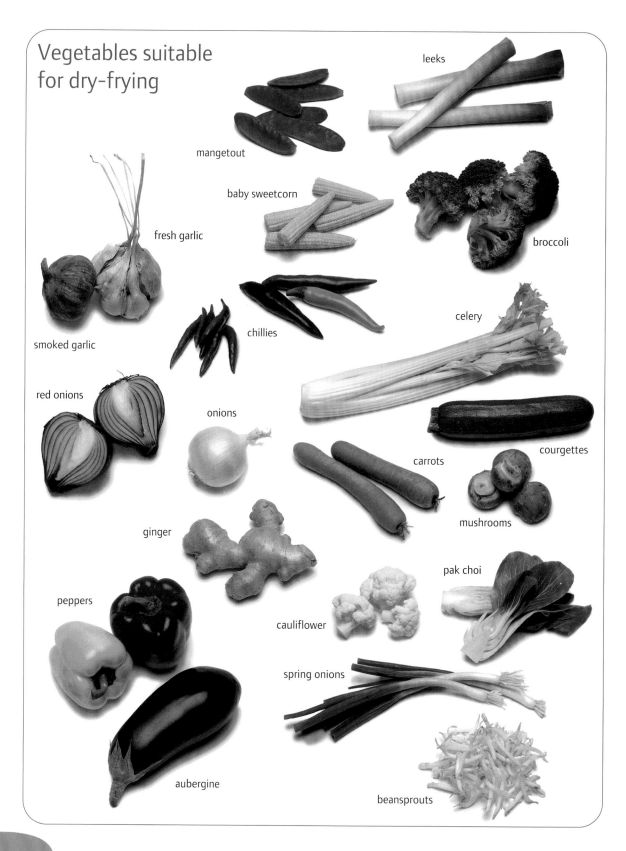

leeks

mangetout

baby sweetcorn

fresh garlic

broccoli

smoked garlic

chillies

celery

red onions

onions

carrots

courgettes

mushrooms

ginger

pak choi

peppers

cauliflower

spring onions

aubergine

beansprouts

Stir-fried mushrooms and peppers

A colourful side dish suitable for meat or fish. For added flavour add 1–2 crushed garlic cloves to the pan during cooking.

Serves 4
1 serving 46 kcal/0.7g fat
Preparation time 20 minutes
Cooking time 10 minutes

2 red and 2 yellow peppers
225g (8oz) button mushrooms
zest and juice of 1 lemon
1 tbsp light soy sauce
1 tbsp chopped fresh chives

1 Prepare the peppers by slicing in half lengthways. Remove the central core and seeds. Cut the peppers into 2.5cm (1in) dice and place in a bowl. Rinse the mushrooms, dry on a piece of kitchen paper and add to the bowl.

2 Pour the lemon zest and juice and the soy sauce over and toss well to coat the vegetables. Heat a non-stick wok or pan until hot. Add the vegetables and cook quickly over a high heat, tossing them so that they cook evenly.

3 Pile into a serving dish and sprinkle with chopped chives.

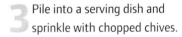

Creamed carrots and swede with cumin

You can make this vegetable side dish in advance and reheat in a moderate oven – cover the dish with baking foil to prevent it from drying out.

Serves 4
1 serving 112 kcal/1.4g fat
Preparation time 15 minutes
Cooking time 30 minutes

1kg (2lb) swede
450g (1lb) carrots, chopped
1 tbsp vegetable bouillon
    powder or 1 vegetable stock
    cube
1 tsp cumin seeds
2 tbsps low-fat fromage frais
salt and freshly ground black
    pepper
fresh parsley to garnish

1 Using a heavy chopping knife, cut the swede into quarters. Peel the swede with a small paring knife and place on a chopping board.

2 Chop the swede into cubes and place in a saucepan with the carrots, bouillon powder or stock cube and cumin seeds and just cover with water. Bring the water to the boil and simmer until the swede and carrots are tender. Drain the swede through a colander and return to the saucepan.

3 Using a potato masher or large fork, mash the swede well until smooth, adding the fromage frais. Season well with salt and pepper and pile into a vegetable serving dish.

4 Garnish with fresh parsley before serving.

Minted peas with turnips

Baby turnips have a distinctive flavour which is at its best when they are just cooked and still a little crisp. Overcooking them can cause them to taste bitter.

Serves 4
1 serving 82 kcal/1.9g fat
Preparation time 20 minutes
Cooking time 20 minutes

450g (1lb) fresh or frozen petits pois
3 garlic cloves, crushed
2 vegetable stock cubes
225g (8oz) baby turnips, washed
4 spring onions, finely sliced
3–4 sprigs fresh mint, chopped
freshly ground black pepper

1 Place the peas, garlic and 1 stock cube in a saucepan. Cover with water and bring to the boil. Simmer for 5–6 minutes until cooked.

2 Place the turnips in a separate saucepan with the other stock cube, cover with boiling water and simmer gently for 5–6 minutes until just tender.

3 Drain both vegetables into a colander. Add the onions and mint, seasoning to taste, and mix together.

4 Spoon onto a serving plate and serve.

Jerusalem artichoke gratin

Jerusalem artichokes offer an alternative to potatoes. They have a distinctive sweet flavour and firm texture.

Serves 4
1 serving 140 kcal/2.8g fat
Preparation time 20 minutes
Cooking time 65 minutes

1kg (2lb) Jerusalem artichokes
1 medium onion, finely sliced
1 garlic clove, crushed
a little grated fresh nutmeg
2 tsps vegetable bouillon stock
    powder
50g (2oz) grated low-fat cheese
600ml (1 pint) skimmed milk
freshly ground black pepper
1 tbsp chopped fresh chives to
    garnish

1 Preheat the oven to 200C, 400F, Gas Mark 6.

2 Scrub the artichokes well, then thinly slice into a large bowl. Add the onion and garlic along with the nutmeg and a little freshly ground black pepper. Add the stock powder and mix together well. Layer into a lightly greased ovenproof dish and cover with grated cheese.

3 Heat the milk in a saucepan and pour over the artichokes.

4 Bake in the centre of the oven for 60 minutes until soft.

5 Sprinkle with chopped chives and serve immediately.

Creamed potatoes

Serves 4
1 serving 100 kcal/0.8g fat
Preparation time 15 minutes
Cooking time 20 minutes

450g (1lb) potatoes, peeled
1 vegetable stock cube
1–2 tbsps low-fat natural yogurt
    or fromage frais
salt and freshly ground black
    pepper

GARLIC MASH
Add 1–2 crushed garlic cloves
to the above and mix well.
1 serving: 100 kcal/0.8g fat

1 Cook the potatoes in boiling water with the vegetable stock cube, then drain well.

2 Mash until smooth, using a potato masher or large fork. Season well with salt and black pepper.

3 Add the yogurt or fromage frais. Mix in well and serve.

CHOOSING POTATOES

There are many varieties of potatoes available virtually all year round. Choosing a suitable variety for a certain style of recipe can be quite daunting.

Charlotte Small round smooth skin potatoes. Ideal for boiling and also dry-frying in a non-stick pan. Great eaten cold in salads.

Cara Large white skin and flesh with pink eyes. Good for jacket potatoes, oven-baked potato wedges, fat-free chips.

King Edward and Red Oval or kidney-shaped white skin with pink colouration – best for mashing or dry-roasting.

Maris Piper Oval with cream-coloured skin – these are one of the most popular varieties. Best for baking, roasting and mashing.

DUCHESSE

Place the yogurt-creamed potatoes in a large piping bag with a large star nozzle. Pipe pyramid shapes onto a non-stick baking tray. Place in a hot oven or under a preheated grill to brown.

1 serving: 100 kcal/0.8g fat

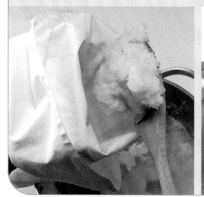

MARQUISE

Pipe potato nests onto a non-stick baking tray. Chop 1 skinned and seeded tomato and mix with a small chopped onion and some freshly chopped basil. Spoon into the centre of each potato nest and bake or grill until brown.

1 serving: 110 kcal/0.9g fat

BOULANGERE

Thinly slice 4 baking potatoes and place in a roasting tray with layers of finely sliced onion. Cover with vegetable stock and bake in a preheated oven at 200C, 400F, Gas Mark 6 for 40 minutes until cooked.

1 serving: 90 kcal/0.3g fat

Dry-roast potatoes

Serves 6
1 serving 90 kcal/0.9g fat
Preparation time 20 minutes
Cooking time 60 minutes

450g (1lb) potatoes, peeled
1 vegetable stock cube
1 tbsp soy sauce, diluted in 2
    tbsps of water (optional)

1 Preheat the oven to 200C,
400F, Gas Mark 6.

2 Cut the potatoes in half and place in a pan of cold, salted water. Bring to the boil, add the stock cube and blanch for 5 minutes.

3 Drain and place on a non-stick baking tray, making sure the potatoes sit curved side down, and baste with the soy sauce mix, if desired.

4 Place in the top of the oven and cook for 60 minutes until golden brown. If the potatoes look too dry during cooking, baste again.

Garlic and herb roasted potatoes

This is a great way to infuse potatoes with garlic. The roasted cloves are delicious yet still pungent when eaten whole.

Serves 4
1 serving 89 kcal/0.4g fat
Preparation time 15 minutes
Cooking time 45 minutes

450g (1lb) charlotte potatoes
8 garlic cloves with skin intact
2–3 sprigs fresh rosemary
2–3 sprigs fresh thyme
2 tbsps reduced-salt soy sauce
chopped fresh flat leaf parsley to
** garnish**

FAT-FREE OVEN CHIPS

For fat-free oven-baked chips, cut potatoes into thick chips or wedges. Boil in water containing a vegetable stock cube for 10 minutes. Drain and place on a non-stick baking tray and place near the top of a preheated hot oven for 20 minutes until crisp. Serve sprinkled with sea salt and vinegar.

1 Preheat the oven to 200C, 400F, Gas Mark 6.

2 Cook the potatoes in lightly salted boiling water for 10 minutes. Drain and place in a non-stick roasting tin.

3 Dot the garlic and herbs over the potatoes, pulling the herb leaves away from the stems. Drizzle with soy sauce and toss the potatoes to coat them with the mixture.

4 Place in the oven and roast for 35–45 minutes, shaking the pan occasionally to prevent sticking.

5 Transfer to a serving bowl and garnish with the parsley.

Potato and red pepper delmonico

Serves 4
1 serving 265 kcal/1.4g fat
Preparation time 30 minutes
Cooking time 55 minutes

675g (1½lb) potatoes, diced
2 medium onions, finely
    chopped
2 red peppers, seeded and diced
2 garlic cloves, crushed
2 tsps vegetable bouillon
    powder
600ml (1 pint) skimmed milk
2 tbsps chopped fresh chives
50g (2oz) fresh breadcrumbs
salt and freshly ground black
    pepper

Potatoes and peppers make a great alternative side dish. The peppers and milk add sweetness to the potatoes as well as a creamy sauce.

1 Preheat the oven to 190C, 375F, Gas Mark 5.

2 In an ovenproof dish place alternate layers of potato, onion, red pepper and garlic, finishing with a layer of potato.

3 Sprinkle with the bouillon powder and season with black pepper. Pour the milk over and sprinkle with the chopped chives.

4 Cover the top with breadcrumbs and season well with salt and black pepper. Bake in the centre of the oven for 45–55 minutes until the potatoes are soft.

5 Serve hot from the oven.

Gratin potatoes with pancetta

These creamy layered potatoes look and taste just like the
real thing but with less than half the fat.

Serves 4
1 serving 290 kcal/4.6g fat
Preparation time 20 minutes
Cooking time 65 minutes

1kg (2lb) potatoes, peeled
1 medium onion, finely sliced
1 garlic clove, crushed
50g (2oz) pancetta or smoked
  bacon
a little grated fresh nutmeg
freshly ground black pepper
2 tsps vegetable bouillon stock
  powder
50g (2oz) grated low-fat cheese
600ml (1 pint) skimmed milk
1 tbsp chopped fresh chives

1 Preheat the oven to 200C,
400F, Gas Mark 6.

2 Thinly slice the potatoes into a
large bowl. Add the onion and
garlic.

3 Cut the pancetta into thin strips
and add to the bowl along with
a little freshly grated nutmeg and
freshly ground black pepper.

4 Add the stock powder and mix
together well. Layer into a
lightly greased ovenproof dish and
cover with the grated cheese.

5 Heat the milk in a saucepan,
then pour over the potatoes.

6 Bake in the centre of the oven
for 60 minutes until soft.

7 Sprinkle with chopped chives
and serve immediately.

Turmeric potatoes with pousse

Pousse is a variety of small leaf spinach. The tender leaves take hardly any cooking, so they can be added to the potatoes a few minutes before serving.

Serves 4
1 serving 154 kcal/1.6g fat
Preparation time 25 minutes
Cooking time 40 minutes

2 tsps coriander seeds
1½ tsps ground turmeric
¼ tsp chilli powder
2 large onions, sliced
2 garlic cloves, crushed
450g (1lb) potatoes, peeled and cut into dice
2 tomatoes, chopped
150ml (¼ pint) vegetable stock
225g (8oz) fresh pousse or baby spinach
chopped fresh coriander to garnish

1 Preheat a non-stick pan. Add the coriander seeds and cook over a gentle heat for a few seconds until the seeds begin to pop.

2 Remove the pan from the heat, add the turmeric and chilli powder and mix well. Add the onions and garlic. Cook together for 3-5 minutes, then add the potatoes and cook for a further 2–3 minutes.

3 Add the tomatoes and stock. Cover and cook gently for 20-30 minutes until the potatoes are tender and only a little liquid remains in the pan. Add the pousse, and mix all the ingredients together.

4 Transfer to a hot serving dish and sprinkle with the fresh coriander.

The perfect jacket potato

Scrub the potatoes. Use a fork to pierce all over the skin of each potato. Season well with salt, then bake near the top of oven at 200C, 400F, Gas Mark 6 for 1–1½ hours.

Each potato, approximately 175g (6oz), 228 kcal/0.6g fat

GREAT LOW-FAT POTATO FILLINGS

Try one of these tasty fillings instead of high-fat butter. If you are calorie-counting, always weigh your jacket potato before cooking, as a jacket potato loses water during cooking and so weighs less when served but still contains the same calories.

Cottage cheese with chopped mixed peppers.

Sweetcorn mixed with low-fat fromage frais and chopped fresh mint.

Baked beans mixed with a little curry paste.

Hot chilli tomatoes – grilled fresh tomatoes mixed with chopped fresh chillies and coriander.

Desserts

For those of us with a 'sweet tooth' a meal doesn't seem complete unless we finish off with something sweet. And there is no reason why we shouldn't – even when we are trying to lose weight or just eating healthily.

Most of the calories from traditional puddings come from the fat they contain. Often it is the invisible fat that causes most of the damage – the melted butter holding the biscuit base together in a cheesecake, the butter in the sponge mixture to create treacle pudding, the fat in the pastry of fruit pies and strudel and the multiple high-fat egg yolks that are used in a roulade. Top them all with a good portion of double cream and you are into serious high-calorie, high-fat overload.

The secret of a successful low-fat dessert is to make it taste every bit as creamy as a full-fat version but to use only low-fat ingredients. For instance, both fromage frais (the Normandy variety is smoothest) and low-fat Greek yogurt make ideal substitutes for double and whipping cream. Fatless sponges double up wonderfully for 'regular' sponge puddings. Meringues are fat free and can be 'dressed up' with all kinds of low-fat fillings, and fruity desserts are always welcome to complete a meal, so make good use of seasonal fresh fruits.

Equipment

PARCHMENT BAKING PAPER

Parchment baking paper is quite different from greaseproof paper. It is silicone-coated with a non-stick surface, making it much easier to lift away from cooked food without the need to grease the paper.

Baking tray

Greaseproof paper

Parchment paper

WHISKS

The most efficient method of whisking egg white is with an electric whisk. This gives maximum volume. A hand rotary or metal whisk will work, although it will take considerably longer and result in slightly less volume of meringue.

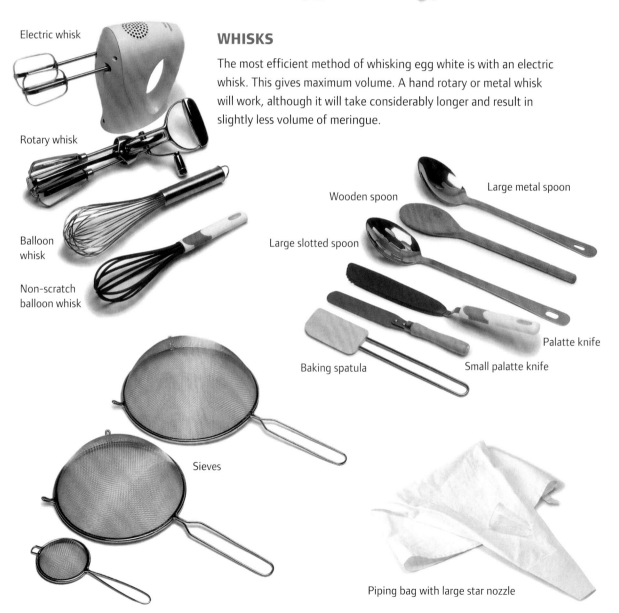

Electric whisk

Rotary whisk

Balloon whisk

Non-scratch balloon whisk

Wooden spoon

Large metal spoon

Large slotted spoon

Palatte knife

Baking spatula

Small palatte knife

Sieves

Piping bag with large star nozzle

How to separate an egg

1 THE SHELL METHOD

1 Crack the shell of the egg at the broadest point by gently tapping it on the side of a small mixing bowl.

2 Holding the egg over the bowl, carefully pull the shell apart, using your thumbs to separate the two halves and allowing some of the egg white to drip down into the bowl beneath.

3 Carefully pass the egg yolk from one half of the egg shell to the other, allowing the egg white to drip down into the bowl beneath.

2 THE SAUCER METHOD

1 Crack the shell of the egg at the broadest point by gently tapping on the side of a saucer.

2 Pull the shell apart and open the egg. Drop the yolk and white onto the saucer.

3 Place a teacup or small bowl over the egg yolk.

4 Holding the cup down, carefully tip the saucer over a small bowl, allowing the white to drip down into the bowl beneath.

CHEF'S TIP

It is important that your mixing bowl and whisk are scrupulously clean, otherwise the egg white will not whisk up fully. Wiping the inside of the bowl first with a piece of freshly cut lemon will help to remove any traces of grease.

Marvellous meringues

Home-baked meringue is very easy to make and tastes fabulous – crunchy on the outside with a mallow chewy centre. Any traces of grease or fat will prevent the egg whites from whisking to their full capacity, so it is really important to separate the yolk fully from the whites. One speck of yolk can ruin many whites.

Makes 8 nests
1 nest 116 kcal/0g fat
Preparation time 10 minutes

4 egg whites
225g (8oz) caster sugar

1 Separate the yolk from the white of 4 eggs one at a time over a small bowl, checking that no yolk drips into the white, then pour into a very clean metal mixing bowl.

2 Whisk the egg whites, using an electric whisk or mixer on full power, until stiff.

LOW-FAT FILLINGS

Fresh fruit Place a spoonful of 0% fat Greek yogurt in the centre of each meringue. Decorate with sliced strawberries and other fruits and a little grated lime zest.

Chocolate au lait Fill each meringue with a dessertspoon of both low-fat vanilla yogurt and low-fat chocolate mousse and dust with cocoa powder.

Banoffi Fill with low-fat toffee yogurt and slices of banana.

3 Using a dessertspoon, add the caster sugar one spoonful at a time at 10-second intervals, keeping the mixer on high speed.

4 Place the mixture in a piping bag with a star tube.

5 Pipe a small disc 5cm (2in) wide onto a baking tray lined with parchment baking paper.

6 Pipe another circle on top of the disc around the outside edge.

7 Pipe other shapes to fill in any gaps left on the baking tray.

8 Bake in a cool oven (140C, 275F, Gas Mark 1) for 3–4 hours until dry on the outside. Turn off the oven and leave the meringues in until cool. When cold, fill the meringues with a selection of low-fat fillings.

FREE FORM MERINGUES

If your kitchen confidence doesn't stretch enough to using a piping bag, spoon the meringue onto the baking parchment paper and make a slight hollow in the centre for the filling after it is cooked. Cook in the same way as piped meringues.

MERINGUE SHAPES

Nests Pipe a small disc (5cm/2in in diameter). Continue to pipe around the outside edge, building up to 4cm (1½in) in height.

Long biscuits Pipe a zig zag 2.5cm (1in) wide and 9cm (3½in) long.

Whirls Pipe small rosette shapes, lifting the nozzle up to a peak. These can be sandwiched together with a little low-fat fromage frais or yogurt.

Meringue roulade

1 Make the meringue as per the recipe and pour into a Swiss roll tin lined with baking parchment.

2 Smooth with a palette knife and bake in a preheated oven (170C, 350F, Gas Mark 3) for 15 minutes.

3 Reduce the temperature of the oven to 150C, 300F, Gas Mark 2, and bake for a further 15 minutes.

4 Turn the meringue out on to a piece of kitchen foil and peel away the parchment paper.

5 Allow to cool, then spread with a thin layer of 0% fat Greek yogurt.

6 Add a few soft berries such as raspberries or sliced strawberries.

7 Roll up the meringue like a Swiss roll, removing the kitchen foil.

8 Place on a serving plate and refrigerate until ready to serve. Just before serving, dust with icing sugar.

Chocolate meringue cherry stacks

Forget chocolate gateau – these meringues taste fantastic. Vary the fruits, using combinations such as raspberries and oranges or kiwi and mango.

Makes 6
1 meringue
   196 kcal/0.8g fat
Preparation time 15
   minutes
Cooking time 3–4
   hours

4 egg whites
225g (8oz) caster
   sugar
2 tsps Valrhona
   cocoa powder,
   sifted
225g (8oz) fresh ripe
   cherries, stoned
   and halved
225g (8oz) 0% fat
   Greek yogurt

Vary your meringues with different flavourings

Coffee Make the basic meringue mix and add 2–3 tsps of instant coffee after all the sugar has been added.

Caramel Make the basic meringue mix, substituting the caster sugar with soft brown sugar. This will make a caramel-flavoured meringue.

Chocolate Make the basic meringue mixture and add 1–2 tsps of Valrhona or dark bitter cocoa powder after the sugar.

1 Preheat the oven to 140C, 275F, Gas Mark 1.

2 In a very clean bowl whisk the egg whites with a mixer until stiff.

3 Using a dessertspoon, add the caster sugar one spoonful at a time at 10-second intervals, keeping the mixer on high speed. Using a large metal spoon, fold in the cocoa powder.

4 Place the mixture in a piping bag with a star tube and pipe small round discs (8cm/4in diameter) onto parchment baking paper or spoon directly onto the paper using a palette knife.

5 Bake in the oven for 3–4 hours until dry on the outside. Turn off the oven and leave the meringues in until cool.

6 Assemble the meringues in layers, sandwiching them together with the yogurt and cherries.

Raspberry baked meringues

Serves 8
1 serving (1 meringue) 116
   kcal/0.04g fat
Preparation time 10 minutes
Cooking time 10 minutes

4 egg whites
225g (8oz) caster sugar
1 vanilla pod
115g (4oz) fresh raspberries
a little icing sugar

Baking meringues with fruit inside adds terrific flavour and texture. They will be crisp on the outside with a chewy concentrated raspberry centre.

1 Preheat the oven to 140C, 275F, Gas Mark 1.

2 In a very clean bowl whisk the egg whites until stiff. Using a dessertspoon, add the caster sugar a spoonful at a time at 10 second intervals, keeping the mixer on high speed.

3 Place the vanilla pod on a chopping board and splice in half lengthways, using a sharp knife. With the blade of the knife, scrape out the seeds from the vanilla pod and add them to the meringue mixture. Place the pod in a storage container filled with sugar (this will flavour the sugar for use in other meringues or desserts).

4 Lightly grease a baking tray and cover with parchment baking paper.

5 Using 2 large spoons, form the meringues into 8 oval shapes by transferring the mixture between the spoons. Place directly onto the paper.

6 Carefully press 4–5 raspberries into the centre of each meringue and smooth over with a knife. Bake in the oven for 3–4 hours until dry on the outside. Turn off the oven and leave the meringues in until cool.

7 Serve with a dusting of icing sugar.

Lemon curd meringue roulade

Lemon meringue without the high-fat pie crust!

Serves 8
1 serving 157 kcal/0.3g fat
Preparation time 10 minutes
Cooking time 30 minutes

for the meringue
4 egg whites
175g (6oz) caster sugar
1 tsp vanilla essence
icing sugar to serve

for the lemon curd
450ml (¾ pint) skimmed
  milk
2 tbsps custard powder
1½ tbsps caster sugar
fine zest and juice of 4
  lemons

1 Preheat the oven to 170C, 350F, Gas Mark 3. Lightly grease and line a large Swiss roll tin with baking parchment.

2 Whisk the egg whites in a dry clean bowl until stiff. Continue whisking, adding the sugar a dessertspoon at a time and allowing 10 seconds between each addition, until all of the sugar is added. Add the vanilla and, using a metal spoon, carefully fold into the mixture.

3 Pour the mixture into the prepared tin and level off with a palette knife. Bake in the oven for 15 minutes.

4 Reduce the oven temperature to 150C, 300F, Gas Mark 2 and bake for a further 15 minutes. Turn the meringue out onto a piece of foil and peel away the parchment. Allow to cool.

5 Meanwhile, make the lemon curd. Heat the milk in a small saucepan until near boiling.

6 In a small bowl, mix the custard powder and sugar with the lemon zest and juice to a smooth paste. Whisk in the hot milk, mix well and return to the pan. Bring back to the boil, whisking continuously until the curd thickens. Allow to cool.

7 When the lemon curd is completely cool, spread evenly over the meringue. Roll up and place on a serving plate. Dust with icing sugar before serving.

Easy fruit fool

Choose a good-quality fromage frais with a rich texture and not too sharp a flavour.
Make this fruit fool in advance and store in the refrigerator until ready to serve.

Serves 4
1 serving 90 kcal/0.4g fat
Preparation time 5 minutes
Cooking time 10 minutes

1 sachet powdered gelatine
450g (16oz) virtually fat-free
Normandy fromage frais
275g (10oz) frozen or fresh
berries, e.g. raspberries,
blackberries, blueberries
2 tbsps Grenadine
caster sugar to taste
3 egg whites
mint and a few raspberries to
decorate

1 Sprinkle the gelatine onto half a cup of boiling water and stir until dissolved. Pour into a small bowl.

2 Place the bowl either over a pan of boiling water or in a microwave for 1 minute until the gelatine is liquid and fully dissolved.

3 Add to the fromage frais and mix together thoroughly.

4 Carefully fold in the raspberries or other fruit and the Grenadine with a little sugar to taste and blend again until combined.

5 Whisk the egg whites until stiff.

6 Fold a third of the whites into the mixture, using a metal spoon. Then fold in the remainder.

7 Spoon into individual glasses or place into a glass bowl and decorate with extra raspberries and mint leaves.

VEGE GEL

A vegetarian alternative to gelatine is available in the form of vege gel. Make up as per packet instructions and use instead of gelatine.

Quick and easy low-fat trifle

Serves 4
1 serving 257 kcal/3.6g fat
Preparation time 5 minutes
Cooking time 10 minutes
Setting time 2–3 hours

4 fat-free trifle sponges
2 tbsps sweet sherry
150g (5oz) fresh strawberries,
  sliced
1 packet strawberry jelly
1 × 75g (3oz) packet instant
  low-fat custard
2 × 150g (2 × 5oz) pots low-fat
  vanilla-flavoured yogurt
extra strawberries to decorate

1 Break the trifle sponges into 4 individual trifle dishes, drizzle with sherry and cover with sliced strawberries.

2 Make up the jelly as per the packet instructions and pour on top.

3 Place in the refrigerator for 2–3 hours until set. Make up the instant custard using boiling water and spoon onto the set jelly.

4 Allow to cool slightly, then cover with the vanilla-flavoured yogurt.

5 Decorate with fresh strawberries and serve.

Strawberry and vanilla parfait

Light evaporated milk forms the base to this luxurious creamy dessert. It is very important that the milk is completely chilled overnight in order to achieve the thick foam once whisked.

Serves 6
1 serving 165 kcal/2.4g fat
Preparation time 15 minutes
Cooking time 5 minutes
Freezing time 4–5 hours

1 × 400g can light evaporated milk, chilled overnight
225g (8oz) fresh strawberries
1 vanilla pod
75g (3oz) caster sugar
225g (8oz) virtually fat-free fromage frais
115g (4oz) Quark (low-fat soft cheese)

1 Using an electric mixer, whisk the evaporated milk on high speed until thick and double in volume.

2 Place the strawberries, reserving a few for decoration, into a liquidiser or food processor and pulse until chopped.

3 Using a sharp knife, split the vanilla pod lengthways, scrape out the black seeds from the centre and add to the strawberries.

4 Mix together the sugar and strawberries, then fold in the milk until fully combined. Carefully fold in the fromage frais and Quark and pour into a plastic freezer container or mould. Cover and freeze for 4–5 hours until firm.

5 Remove from the freezer 10 minutes before serving.

6 Using a serrated knife dipped in boiling water, slice into portions. Decorate with the reserved strawberries.

Strawberries with black pepper and balsamic dressing

Sweet and sour flavours mix together for an unusual dessert. It's best to assemble this dessert just before required, although you can prepare the strawberries in advance and store in the refrigerator.

Serves 4
1 serving 60 kcal/0.1g fat
Preparation time 10 minutes
Cooking time 5 minutes

450g (1lb) fresh strawberries
good pinch of cracked black pepper
2 tbsps dry sherry
1 tbsp good quality balsamic
  vinegar
zest of a lime
1 tbsp icing sugar
300ml (½ pint) 0% fat Greek
  yogurt

1 Wash and hull the strawberries and allow to drain. Using a small knife, cut the strawberries in half, place in a serving dish and sprinkle with the cracked black pepper.

2 In a small bowl mix together the sherry and balsamic vinegar. Pour over the strawberries. Sprinkle with the lime zest and dust with icing sugar.

3 Serve with the yogurt.

Orange and Grand Marnier tiramisu

This is a delicious alternative to the traditional Italian coffee and chocolate dessert. It looks stunning layered in individual glasses or just as impressive in a glass dish as a centrepiece. Although this is a very quick and easy dessert to prepare, you can prepare the oranges in advance if you wish and place in the refrigerator until required.

Serves 4
1 serving 203 kcal/1.1g fat
Preparation time 15 minutes
Cooking time 10 minutes

4 large oranges
300ml (½ pint) fresh orange juice
2 tbsps Grand Marnier or orange liqueur
16 sponge finger biscuits
600ml (1 pint) 0% fat Greek yogurt
1 tsp cocoa powder to dust

1 Prepare the oranges by slicing off the top and bottom of each one. Remove the peel and pith with a sharp knife, cutting around the oranges like a barrel (reserve the peel). Using a sharp knife, segment the oranges into a bowl, cutting in between the thin membrane to give perfect orange segments. Squeeze any juice from the centre core into a separate bowl. Add the fresh orange juice and the Grand Marnier or orange liqueur to the bowl.

2 Start to layer the dessert into 4 individual glasses by soaking each sponge finger in the orange liquid briefly and then placing in the glasses, adding a spoonful of yogurt and a few orange segments between each layer, and finishing with a layer of yogurt. Refrigerate until ready to serve.

3 Place the reserved orange peel, orange side down, on a chopping board. Shave away the pith with a sharp knife. Cut each piece of peel into very thin strips, blanch in boiling water for 5 minutes, drain and allow to cool.

4 Just before serving, dust each tiramisu with cocoa powder and decorate with a pinch of orange zest.

Strawberries poached in Burgundy

 This recipe also works well with frozen strawberries. Make up the hot wine mixture, pour over the frozen berries and allow to cool. Serve with low-fat yogurt or fromage frais.

Serves 4
1 serving 169 kcal/0.09g fat
Preparation time 5 minutes
Cooking time 10 minutes

115g (4oz) demerara sugar
1 cinnamon stick
150ml (¼ pint) Burgundy wine
350g (12oz) fresh small strawberries, hulled and rinsed
mint leaves to decorate

1 In a saucepan dissolve the sugar in 300ml (½ pint) water and bring to the boil, adding the cinnamon stick.

2 Add the Burgundy and bring the mixture to a gentle simmer. Simmer for 10 minutes until the wine has reduced.

3 Remove the pan from the heat and add the strawberries.

4 Pour into a serving bowl and allow to cool. Serve in glass dishes and decorate with mint leaves.

Oranges and passion-fruit in Madeira wine

Serves 4
1 serving 174 kcal/0.3g fat
Preparation time 20 minutes
Cooking time 10 minutes

300ml (½ pint) Madeira wine
1 cinnamon stick
2 tbsps soft brown sugar
4 large fresh oranges
6 large passion-fruits

1 Place the Madeira, cinnamon and sugar in a small saucepan and heat gently until the sugar has dissolved.

2 Using a small serrated knife, slice off the top and bottom of one orange. Stand the orange up on the cut edge and slice away the peel from top to bottom, working around the fruit. Repeat with all the oranges.

3 Cut each orange across in 6 slices but not all the way through so that the orange stays just intact. Arrange the oranges in a serving dish.

4 Cut the passion-fruits in half and scoop out the flesh onto the oranges. Pour the Madeira syrup on top and refrigerate until ready to serve.

5 Serve with low-fat yogurt or virtually fat-free fromage frais.

Orange rice torte

Pour a dash of Grand Marnier orange liqueur over
this delicious cold rice dessert just before serving.

Serves 8
1 serving 212 kcal/0.4g fat
Preparation time 20 minutes
Cooking time 40 minutes
Setting time overnight

150g (5oz) pudding rice
600ml (1 pint) skimmed milk
115g (4oz) caster sugar
4 oranges
6 sheets gelatine
450ml (¾ pint) ready-made
low-fat custard
2 tsps vanilla essence
a few grapes to decorate

1 Place the rice, milk and sugar in a heavy-based saucepan. Bring to a gentle simmer, stirring continuously. Reduce the heat and continue to simmer uncovered for 20 minutes until most of the milk has been absorbed and the rice is cooked.

2 Using a fine grater, remove the zest from 2 of the oranges, place in the saucepan and stir well.

3 Soak the gelatine in a bowl of cold water until soft. Squeeze out the water and place in a small bowl. Dissolve the gelatine either in a microwave for 30 seconds on full power or by sitting the bowl in a large saucepan of boiling water. Beat the gelatine into the rice. Stir in the custard and vanilla.

4 Pour the mixture into a deep round 1.5 litre (3 pint) mould and chill until set, preferably overnight.

5 Cut the skin away from the remaining oranges and cut the oranges into segments.

6 To unmould the dessert, dip the mould in a bowl containing boiling water for 2-3 seconds, and place an upturned serving plate on top. Quickly flip the mould over and remove.

7 Decorate with orange segments and grapes.

Chocolate orange cups

Valrhona cocoa powder is made using a high quantity of cocoa solids, resulting in a much stronger, fuller chocolate flavour. Chocolate cups are available in most supermarkets. They make a perfect container for low-fat fillings or fresh fruit.

Serves 6
1 serving 106 kcal/4g fat
Preparation time 5 minutes
Cooking time 10 minutes

1 × 75g (3oz) packet instant
   chocolate custard
2 tsps bitter cocoa powder
   (Valrhona or Green & Blacks)
1 orange
1 tbsp caster sugar
6 dark chocolate cups
mint to decorate

1 Make up the custard with boiling water as per the packet instructions, stir in the cocoa and allow to cool.

2 Slice the orange in half lengthways, then slice down to give semi-circles. Place the orange pieces in a small saucepan and just cover with boiling water. Add the sugar and simmer over a low heat for 10 minutes until soft. Remove from the heat and allow to cool.

3 Assemble the desserts by filling the cups with the cold custard, then top with 2 slices of orange. Place a third twisted slice of orange on top and decorate with fresh mint. Chill until required.

Blackberry and apple fool

This recipe works better with well ripened fruit. If the fruit is underripe, add to the apples and cook lightly to soften.

Serves 4
1 serving 204 kcal/0.2g fat
Preparation time 15 minutes
Cooking time 20 minutes

225g (8oz) blackberries
225g (8oz) cooking apples
115g (4oz) golden caster sugar
2 tbsps Calvados or brandy
225g (8oz) Quark (low-fat soft cheese)
2 egg whites
fresh mint to decorate

1 Rinse the blackberries under cold water. Peel, core and slice the apples and place in a saucepan. Cook over a low heat until soft, stirring from time to time to prevent sticking.

2 Add the sugar and place over a low heat to reduce to a thick puree. Allow to cool, then mix in the blackberries.

3 Beat in the Quark to a smooth consistency.

4 Whisk the egg whites until they stand in stiff peaks. Gently fold into the fruit puree and sweeten to taste.

5 Spoon into individual glasses and decorate with fresh mint.

Papaya and lime layer

Serves 6
1 serving 150 kcal/2.2g fat
Preparation time 20 minutes

1 large papaya
zest and juice of 1 lime
225g (8oz) low-fat sponge
fingers
2 tbsps dry sherry
2 egg whites
300ml (½ pint) 0% fat Greek
yogurt
2 tbsps icing sugar

Papaya is a deliciously sweet fruit with a soft texture.
Choose ripe fruit with soft, not firm, skin.

1 Prepare the papaya by slicing in half lengthways with a sharp knife. Carefully remove the seeds, using a dessertspoon. Peel away the outer skin slicing around the fruit. Cut the fruit into small pieces and place in a bowl. Add the lime zest and juice.

2 Place the sponge fingers in a food processor and reduce to fine crumbs. Pour into a bowl, sprinkle with the sherry, and set aside.

3 Whisk the egg whites until stiff, then gradually fold in the yogurt and icing sugar.

4 Assemble the dessert in a glass dish in layers, first with the sponge finger crumbs sprinkled with sherry, then papaya and finally the yogurt mixture. Repeat, dusting the top with crumbs.

5 Refrigerate until ready to serve.

Fresh lemon jelly

This citrus dessert is really great – full of flavour, with virtually no fat at all.

Serves 4
1 serving 209 kcal/0.1g fat
Preparation time 5 minutes
Cooking time 20 minutes

150g (5oz) caster sugar
2–3 sprigs lemon balm or fresh
  mint
zest of 2 lemons
900ml (2 pints) water
75g (3oz) cornflour
juice of 6 lemons
fresh mint leaves to decorate

1 In a saucepan heat the sugar, lemon balm or mint, zest and water until boiling. Remove the lemon balm leaves (if using).

2 Slake the cornflour with a little cold water and mix to a smooth paste.

3 Stir into the hot water. Bring to the boil, stirring continuously. Stir in the juice of 3 lemons and continue boiling for a further 2 minutes.

4 Allow to cool completely. Pour into a food processor or blender and blend, adding the remaining lemon juice. Pour the mixture into serving dishes and place in the refrigerator overnight.

5 Decorate with fresh mint leaves and serve.

Low-fat pancakes

This recipe makes 8 pancakes, allowing 2 pancakes per person. The oil is needed for frying the pancakes to give them a little crispness, but most of it is removed with the kitchen paper before cooking.

Serves 4
1 serving 157 kcal/
    4.9g fat
Preparation time
    15 minutes
Cooking time
    15 minutes

115g (4oz) plain flour
pinch of salt
1 egg
300ml (½ pint)
    skimmed or semi-
    skimmed milk
4 tsps vegetable oil

1 Sift the flour with the salt in a bowl and, using a metal spoon, draw the flour to the sides of the bowl to make a well in the centre.

2 Pour the egg into the well and very carefully stir into the flour with a wooden spoon.

3 Slowly add half the milk, stirring continuously. Mix until smooth.

4 Add the remaining milk and beat well with a whisk.

5 Cover and leave the mixture to stand for 20–30 minutes. The batter should be the consistency of thick cream.

6 Preheat a non-stick frying pan with 1 tsp of oil.

CHEF'S TIP

When using eggs in cooking, always crack them first into a cup or bowl to check that they have not gone off and to check that no shell has broken into them.

7 Wipe out the pan with kitchen paper, taking care not to burn your fingers (wear an oven glove if necessary).

8 Take 2 tbsps of batter for each pancake. Tilt the pan as you pour in the batter so that the batter spreads evenly across the bottom of the pan.

9 Cook until the underneath of the pancake is a golden brown colour. Slide, a non-stick spatula underneath the pancake to loosen it, and give the pan a shake to make sure the pancake is completely loose.

10 Flip the pancake over and cook for about 15 seconds on the other side, then remove from the pan and keep warm. Repeat until you have 8 pancakes, adding a tsp of oil to the pan and wiping out after every 2 pancakes.

11 Serve immediately with fresh orange or lemon juice and honey or brown sugar.

EGGS

Egg white is very low in fat and very high in protein. In a size 2 egg, the egg white yields only 15 kcal, no fat and 3.5g protein. The egg yolk, on the other hand, is high in fat. One egg yolk contains 75 kcal, 6.6g fat and 4g protein.

Size 1	98 kcal per egg	7.3g fat per egg	8.2g protein per egg
Size 2	90 kcal per egg	6.6g fat per egg	7.5g protein per egg
Size 3	84 kcal per egg	6.2g fat per egg	7g protein per egg

Ginger and blueberry crème brûlée

A great combination of fruit and spice with a luxurious creamy topping.

Serves 4
1 serving 160 kcal/1.3g fat
Preparation time 10 minutes
Cooking time 5 minutes

2 tbsps stem ginger
225g (8oz) blueberries
450g 0% fat Greek yogurt
4 tbsps demerara sugar

1 Slice the stem ginger and place in a small saucepan. Add the blueberries. Place over a low heat until the fruit starts to pop. Spoon into 4 ramekin dishes and chill.

2 When the fruit is chilled, preheat the grill until it is very hot. Just before you are ready to serve, spread the yogurt over the fruit, covering the fruit completely.

3 Sprinkle with the sugar and immediately place under the grill until the sugar caramelises.

4 Serve straight away or allow to cool and serve cold.

Pear and lemon brûlée

This luxurious dessert can be made in advance and kept in the refrigerator until ready to serve. It is important to add the sugar just before grilling as it will start to dissolve on contact with the yogurt.

Serves 4
1 serving 215 kcal/1.3g fat
Preparation time 10 minutes
Cooking time 20 minutes

2 lemons
2 ripe dessert pears
2 tbsps caster sugar
450g (16oz) 0% fat Greek yogurt
4 tbsps demerara sugar

1 Using the fine side of a grater, finely grate the lemons into a small bowl. Cut the lemons in half, squeeze out the juice and place in the bowl.

2 Cut the pears in quarters, remove the centre cores and the peel. Place the quartered pears in the bowl, turning them to coat with the lemon juice to prevent them from discolouring.

3 Tip the lemons into a saucepan and add 300ml (½ pint) of water and the caster sugar. Bring to the boil, then reduce the heat and simmer gently for 10–15 minutes until the pears are soft.

4 Lift the pears from the syrup and place on a chopping board. Slice thinly and place in the bottom of 4 ramekin dishes. Cover with yogurt and smooth the tops with a knife. Place in the refrigerator until ready to serve.

5 Preheat the grill until it is very hot. Just before you are ready to serve, sprinkle the brûlées with the demerara sugar and immediately place under the hot grill until the sugar caramelises. Serve immediately.

Golden lemon pudding

Serves 4
1 serving 262 kcal/0.8g fat
Preparation time 5 minutes
Cooking time 25 minutes

3 tbsps light brown sugar

4 egg whites

3 tbsps low-fat fromage frais

3 tbsps flour

2 tbsps fine cornmeal (polenta flour)

2 tsps baking powder

3 tbsps lemon marmalade

This mixture makes a good-sized pudding, ideal to follow a light lunch or dinner.

1 In a mixing bowl combine the sugar, egg white and fromage frais and beat well. Fold in the flours and baking powder.

2 Lightly grease a 600ml (1 pint) pudding basin with a little vegetable oil. Place the lemon marmalade in the bottom of the bowl and pour the mixture over. Cover the basin with food wrap. Place in a steamer over a pan of boiling water and steam for 20 minutes or until the pudding is cooked.

3 Carefully remove the basin from the steamer and run a palate knife around the edge of the bowl to loosen the pudding. Turn the pudding out onto a plate and serve with either low-fat fromage frais or low-fat custard.

Sticky Valrhona chocolate and pear pudding

Serves 8
1 serving 162 kcal/2.9g fat
Preparation time 10 minutes
Cooking time 35 minutes

for the sponge
75g (3oz) plain flour
25g (1oz) Valrhona cocoa
 powder
1 tsp baking powder
115g (4oz) caster sugar
115g (4oz) virtually fat-free
 fromage frais
2 eggs
a little oil
2 poached cooked pears or
 1 × 400g can pears in natural
 juice, cut into quarters

for the topping
200ml (7fl oz) boiling water
2 tbsps Valrhona cocoa powder
2 tbsps soft dark brown sugar
fromage frais to serve

1 Preheat the oven to 180C, 350F, Gas Mark 5. Sieve together the flour, cocoa powder and baking powder.

2 In a mixing bowl beat together the sugar, fromage frais and eggs.

3 Gradually mix in the sifted ingredients.

4 Pour the mixture into a lightly greased 1 litre (2 pint) ovenproof dish.

5 Combine the topping ingredients, pour over the sponge mixture and cook in the centre of the oven for 35 minutes.

6 Remove from the oven, place the pear quarters on top and return to the oven for 5 minutes more to heat through.

7 Dust with a little icing sugar and serve
hot with virtually fat-free fromage frais.

Grilled spiced nectarines

Serves 4
1 serving 149 kcal/0.3g fat
Preparation time 10 minutes
Cooking time 5 minutes

4 large nectarines
1 large orange
1 tbsp stem ginger in syrup,
  chopped
1 tsp ground cinnamon
6 cardamom pods, crushed with
  seeds removed
4 tsps light muscovado sugar

This dessert is very flexible; either cook, chill and serve cold or prepare to the point of cooking and grill just prior to serving.

1 Preheat the grill to high.

2 Cut each nectarine in half, remove the centre stone, and place each half on a non-stick baking tray. Using a zester, zest the orange peel into a small bowl. Cut the orange in half and squeeze out the juice into the bowl.

3 Drain the syrup from the ginger into the bowl and finely chop the ginger and add to the bowl, along with the spices. Mix together well, then spoon onto the nectarines.

4 Sprinkle with sugar and place immediately under a hot grill for 3–4 minutes until the sugar has caramelised and the nectarines are soft.

5 Serve piping hot with virtually fat-free fromage frais.

Baked pumpkin pudding

An interesting way to serve pumpkin. Serve the puddings straight from the oven lightly dusted with icing sugar.

Serves 4
1 serving 223 kcal/3.5g fat
Preparation time 20 minutes
Cooking time 40 minutes

450g (1lb) fresh pumpkin, peeled and diced
2 tbsps red wine
2 tsps mixed spice
2 eggs
3½ tbsps dark brown sugar
1 level tbsp self-raising flour
300ml (½ pint) skimmed milk
1 tsp vanilla extract

1 Preheat the oven to 200C, 400F, Gas Mark 6.

2 Lightly grease 4 individual ramekin dishes or an ovenproof dish.

3 Place the pumpkin in the bottom of a saucepan and add 2 tbsps of water. Cook over a low heat for 10 minutes to soften the pumpkin, adding a little more water if required.

4 When the pumpkin has softened, stir in the red wine and continue cooking until all the wine has been absorbed.

5 In a mixing bowl beat together the mixed spice, eggs and sugar until thick and creamy. Gradually blend in the flour to a smooth paste, adding a little milk if necessary. Stir in the cooked pumpkin.

6 Heat the milk with the vanilla in a small saucepan until near boiling.

7 Slowly pour the milk onto the batter, stirring continuously. Spoon the batter into the prepared dish or dishes. Stand the dishes in a roasting tin and pour in sufficient boiling water to come halfway up the sides. Bake in the oven for 25–30 minutes until set.

8 Serve warm with low-fat fromage frais.

Apple and sultana strudel

Apple pie without the high-fat crust. This strudel will freeze well as a whole dessert or you can slice it into portions and reheat from frozen. Allow 30 minutes if cooking from frozen. Serve with virtually fat-free fromage frais.

Serves 8
1 serving 120 kcal/1.4g fat
Preparation time 20 minutes
Cooking time 40 minutes

4 large cooking apples
6 sheets filo pastry
   (30cm × 20cm/12in × 8in)
1 egg, beaten
2 tbsps demerara sugar
75g (3oz) sultanas
2 tsps ground cinnamon
icing sugar to dust

1 Preheat the oven to 200C, 400F, Gas Mark 6. Lightly grease a non-stick baking tray with sunflower oil spray. Peel, core and slice the apples into a large bowl of salted water. This will help to prevent the apples from turning brown. Rinse the apples well in fresh cold water and place in a large saucepan. Cook over a low heat for 15-20 minutes until soft. Spoon into a bowl and allow to cool.

2 Separate the filo pastry sheets. Place one onto a tea towel and brush with beaten egg. Continue adding the remaining sheets, brushing each layer with egg.

3 Spread the cooked apple over the pastry leaving a 2.5cm (1in) border around the edge. Sprinkle with the sugar and sultanas and dust with the cinnamon.

4 Fold in the two short sides of the pastry.

5 Roll up the pastry like a Swiss roll and place on the prepared non-stick baking tray. Brush the top with egg and bake in the oven for 20 minutes until crisp and golden.

6 Remove from the oven. Cut into slices and serve hot with a dusting of icing sugar.

Apple and blackberry turnovers

Makes 8 parcels
1 parcel 116 kcal/1.4g fat
Preparation time 20 minutes
Cooking time 40 minutes

2 large cooking apples
juice of ½ lemon
2 tbsps caster sugar
115g (4oz) blackberries
1 egg
3 tbsps skimmed milk
8 sheets filo pastry
1 tsp granulated sugar
icing sugar to dust

Here, this traditional sweet pie filling is made light and low-fat. These taste just as good cold with a little low-fat yogurt or fromage frais.

1 Preheat the oven to 200C, 400F, Gas Mark 6.

2 Peel and core the apples and place in a saucepan with the lemon juice and caster sugar. Cook over a low heat until the apple has cooked down to a pulp. Allow to cool, then stir in the blackberries.

3 Beat together the egg and milk. Take one sheet of filo pastry and brush with the egg mixture. Fold a third of the long side into the centre and again on the other side to leave a long strip of pastry. Brush again with egg, then place a good tbsp of the fruit mixture at one end of the pastry and fold over diagonally, enclosing the mixture in a triangle. Fold the pastry back over along the length of the pastry, retaining the triangle shape and tucking in any spare ends. Brush with egg, place on a baking tray, and dust lightly with granulated sugar. Repeat this process for all 8 parcels.

4 Bake in the oven for 15–20 minutes until golden brown. Dust with icing sugar and serve hot with any leftover filling and low-fat custard.

Griddled pineapple with jerk seasoning

Jerk seasoning is a blend of spices usually coupled with savoury items. The spices have been adapted to work as a spice mix for a sweet dessert.

Serves 4
1 serving 84 kcal/0.3g fat
Preparation time 10 minutes
Cooking time 10 minutes

1 large fresh pineapple
½ tsp ground allspice
1 tsp finely chopped fresh
  ginger
¼ tsp ground mace
1 tsp finely chopped lemongrass
zest and juice of a lime
1 tbsp runny honey
2 tbsps chopped fresh coriander

1 Prepare the pineapple by slicing off the top and bottom with a sharp knife. Remove the outer skin, slicing down and around the fruit. Cut across the fruit to make slices 2.5cm (1in) thick and place in a shallow dish. Leaving the central core in will help hold the slices together during cooking.

2 Mix together the remaining ingredients, except the coriander, and spoon over the pineapple.

3 Preheat a griddle pan or health grill until hot. Cook the pineapple briefly on each side for 1–2 minutes, taking care not to allow the honey to burn.

4 Sprinkle with chopped coriander before serving.

Hot chestnut pudding with rum sauce

A nutty sponge pudding that is low in fat. Make in advance and reheat in a steamer just before serving.

Serves 6
1 serving 261 kcal/2.9g fat
Preparation time 10 minutes
Cooking time 20 minutes

115g (4oz) cooked apple purée
115g (4oz) dark brown sugar
175g (6oz) plain flour, sifted
with 1 tsp baking powder
2 eggs, beaten
2 tsps ground ginger
2 tsps ground cinnamon
50g (2oz) cooked chopped
chestnuts

for the sauce
300ml (½ pint) semi-skimmed
milk
1 vanilla pod, split
2 tsps arrowroot
2 tbsps rum
sugar to taste

1 Preheat the oven to 180C, 350F, Gas Mark 4.

2 Prepare 6 individual (115g/4oz) ramekins or a 12cm (6in) square cake tin by lightly greasing with a little margarine then dusting with a little flour.

3 In a large mixing bowl, mix together the apple purée and sugar, using a wooden spoon. Add the flour and eggs a little at a time, beating well between each addition. Fold in the spices and chestnuts and spoon into the ramekins.

4 Bake in the oven for 20 minutes until well risen.

5 Make the sauce by heating the milk and vanilla pod until near boiling. Slake the arrowroot with a little cold milk or water and whisk into the milk. Add the rum and simmer gently for 2–3 minutes to allow the sauce to thicken. Sweeten to taste with a little sugar.

6 If making individual puddings, turn out onto a plate, or cut the square pudding into pieces, and coat with the sauce.

Barbecues

Everybody loves a barbecue. It's fun to cook outside on a sunny day and the preparation of the meal often involves the whole family.

Barbecuing is excellent for anyone wanting to eat low fat, as it encourages the fat to drip away from the food, rather like a grill, except that the heat is coming from below rather than above. Remember, for every 28 grams (1oz) of fat that drips away you are saving yourself 252 calories of fat!

This fast method of cooking can be applied to a variety of foods from sausages, steaks and chops to vegetables, fish and many types of fruits. The key is to substitute fat with flavour. Freshly ground black pepper is the easiest way to make a difference but try other seasonings, too, such as tandoori or korma curry powder to add some spice.

Equipment

There are many designs of barbecues or charcoal grills on the market with many different uses in mind. Check which ones will suit your lifestyle. Choose one that has a lid to ensure maximum control over the heat. It can also greatly reduce flare-ups by minimising the draughts, reducing the risk of excess flames that burn and dry up the food being cooked. You will also need some special long-handled utensils to enable you to move food around safely.

CHOOSING A BARBECUE

There are two main types of barbecues to choose from – charcoal or gas. The secret of successful barbecuing is ensuring the coals are hot enough before starting to cook. A gas barbecue needs less time to warm up.

CHARCOAL

Benefits: traditional authentic flavours coupled with the fun factor 'hands on' cooking experience.

Disadvantages: dirty to handle. Damp fuel will cause poor ignition.

GAS

Benefits: easy ignition, instant cooking, controllable heat settings, cheaper to run, clean and efficient.

Disadvantages: reduced traditional smoky flavour and less fun!

BARBECUE TOOLS

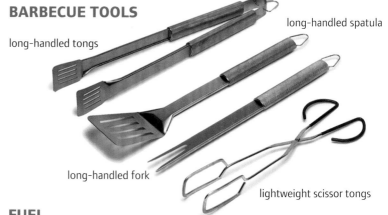

long-handled tongs

long-handled spatula

long-handled fork

lightweight scissor tongs

FUEL

Choose smokeless, environmentally safe, food-related fuel. This will guarantee a long high temperature without any nasty chemicals to impair the flavour of the food. Before lighting the barbecue, lightly oil the cooking rack – this will burn off before the food is placed onto the rack but will help to prevent the food from sticking.

FLAVOURED CHIPS

There are many different types of flavoured wooden chips from hickory, apple, alder and cherry. These add a distinctive flavour to the food being cooked. To use, sprinkle around the perimeter of the hot coals and allow the smoke to season the food.

CLEANING

Barbecue brushes help to remove any residue or stubborn baked-on food. After cleaning, brush lightly with vegetable oil. This will help to prevent rust forming and it will be burnt off the next time the barbecue is lit.

Barbecue cooking tips

Prawns Whole prawns are ideal for barbecues. Always make sure they are hot right through to the centre. As they cook they change colour from blue/grey to bright pink, which is a good indication of visually checking they are cooked.

Chicken, poultry and pork These need to be fully cooked. Always insert a knife into the thickest part of the drumstick or fillet. The flesh should be white, not pink and wet. Even if the outer meat looks well done, always check that the inside is fully cooked before serving.

Beef and lamb Cut steaks and slices no thicker than 2.5cm (1in) to ensure quick and effective cooking. Thick pieces of meat can be made thinner by wrapping in a food bag and beating with a rolling pin. Can be served slightly pink.

Fish As well as fish kebabs, some dense fish such as tuna and swordfish steaks can be cooked very easily directly on the barbecue grid. Whole round fish such as trout, whiting or small salmon need to be cooked either in a lightly oiled wire grid or wrapped in foil to prevent the fish from falling apart during cooking.

TIMING

It is essential to cook food in the right order to ensure your collection of food is perfectly cooked and piping hot when ready to serve. As you add more food to the barbecue move the cooked food to the outside edge where the heat is not as fierce as the centre. Vegetables can be kept warm by wrapping in kitchen foil.

1st jacket potatoes
2nd meat products
3rd fish products
4th vegetables

Scallops wrapped in Parma ham with sweet chilli dip

Scallops make a fantastic barbecue starter. They take just minutes to cook and taste really good. Other chunky fish such as monkfish work just as well.

Serves 4
1 serving 148 kcal/4g fat
Preparation time 15 minutes
Cooking time 5 minutes

12 large fresh scallops
6 slices Parma ham
1 lemon or lime, cut into wedges
salt and freshly ground black
    pepper

for the dipping sauce
1 red chilli, finely sliced
2 tbsps rice wine vinegar
2 tsps caster sugar
1 tsp chopped fresh lemongrass

1. Prepare the scallops by cleaning well under a cold running tap to remove any sand or grit. Pull away the small membrane attached to the side, taking care to keep the orange coral intact. Pat dry with kitchen paper and season well with salt and black pepper.

2. Trim away any fat from the Parma ham and cut each slice in half lengthways.

3. Wrap each scallop with a strip of Parma ham and place on a wooden or metal skewer with a wedge of lemon or lime.

4. Mix together all the dipping sauce ingredients in a bowl.

5. Place the scallops on a hot barbecue and cook for 2–3 minutes, turning constantly.

6. Serve hot straight away with the dipping sauce.

Chicken and chorizo sticks

Serves 4
1 serving 89 kcal/3.8g fat
Preparation time 10 minutes
Cooking time 10 minutes

1 skinless chicken breast
8 thin slices chorizo sausage
2 tbsps light soy sauce
zest and juice of 1 lime
freshly ground black pepper

Chorizo is a Spanish pork sausage highly spiced with paprika.
Although it contains fat, some will remove during cooking.

1 Cut the chicken into bite-sized pieces. Place in a shallow dish and
season well with black pepper. Combine the soy sauce with the lime
and pour over the chicken.

2 Take 8 wooden cocktail sticks and thread alternate pieces of chicken
and chorizo onto the sticks.

3 Place the sticks on a hot barbecue and cook for 2–3 minutes on each
side until the chicken is fully cooked. Serve hot or cold.

Main courses

Tandoori beef and mushroom burgers

Home-made burgers are fantastic cooked on a barbecue, as it gives them a smoky roasted flavour. When moulding them together, flatten them with the palm of your hands, as the depth is very important to the cooking time. If the burgers are too thick they will take much longer to cook through to the centre, causing the outside to overcook or even burn.

Makes 8 burgers
1 burger 133 kcal/5g fat
Preparation time 20 minutes
Cooking time 20–25 minutes

450g (1lb) extra lean minced
  beef
1 medium red onion, finely
  chopped
2 garlic cloves, crushed
225g (8oz) chestnut mushrooms,
  finely chopped
1 tbsp tandoori curry powder
2 tsps vegetable bouillon stock
  powder
1 tbsp chopped fresh mixed
  herbs (parsley, chives,
  oregano)
50g (2oz) fresh breadcrumbs
freshly ground black pepper

1 In a large mixing bowl combine the beef, onion, garlic and mushrooms.

2 Work the mixture with 2 forks to break up the meat and mix well.

3 Sprinkle the tandoori powder and bouillon stock powder over and stir in well, making sure it is fully combined throughout.

4 Add the herbs and breadcrumbs and season with plenty of freshly ground black pepper.

5 Mix thoroughly. Using a metal spoon, bring the mixture together.

6 Divide the mixture into 8 equal-sized balls, then squeeze each one between your hands to flatten. Set aside.

7 Cook on a hot barbecue for 10 minutes on each side. Check that the burgers are cooked by pulling one apart to check the centre is fully cooked. If in doubt return to the barbecue or grill for a further 5–10 minutes.

Indian pork burgers

These meaty nibbles make ideal party food. Children love them as well as grown-ups. You could substitute minced turkey or chicken for the pork. Try to hunt out green cardamom in your local supermarket spice range. To use, crush the pods with a broad edge of a chopping knife and remove the seeds. Discard the pods and either crush the seeds in a pestle and mortar or add whole.

Makes 8 burgers
1 burger 202 kcal/8g fat
Preparation time 15 minutes
Cooking time 30 minutes

1kg (2lb) lean minced pork
1 red onion, finely chopped
2 garlic cloves, crushed
2 tsps ground coriander
2 tsps ground cumin
8 cardamom pods, crushed and
    seeds removed
pinch of dried chilli flakes
1 tbsp mango chutney
2 tbsps chopped fresh parsley
1 tsp salt
1 tbsp tomato purée

1 Place all the ingredients in a large bowl and mix well. Mould the mixture into 8 burgers, and place on a non-stick baking tray. Cover with food wrap and refrigerate until ready to cook.

2 Cook on a hot barbecue for 25–30 minutes. Serve hot.

VARY YOUR HOME-MADE BURGERS

Turkey korma burgers Use recipe as on page 240, but use minced turkey and mild korma curry powder instead of the tandoori mix.   **Per burger 95 kcal/0.8g fat**

Minted lamb burgers Use lean minced lamb and add 2 tbsps of finely chopped fresh mint.   **Per burger 144 kcal/7g fat**

Vegetarian burgers Substitute 450g (1lb) soya mince. Add 1 finely diced red pepper. After moulding, refrigerate for at least 1 hour before cooking.   **Per burger 186 kcal/3.4g fat**

Lamb koftas with creamy chilli dip

This is great way to serve lean minced lamb. It also works well for chicken or turkey.
These slim kebabs will cook much quicker than sausages or burgers.

Serves 4
1 serving 244 kcal/16g fat
Preparation time 20 minutes
Cooking time 10 minutes

450g (1lb) lean minced lamb
1 smoked garlic clove, crushed
1 tbsp finely chopped fresh mint
1 tbsp finely chopped fresh flat
   leaf parsley
1 tsp ground cumin
1 tsp ground turmeric
1 tsp ground allspice
1 egg beaten
salt and freshly ground black
   pepper

for the chilli dip
1 small pot low-fat yogurt
1 smoked garlic clove, crushed
1–2 tsps chilli paste
1 tbsp finely chopped fresh mint

1 In a large bowl mix together the lamb mince, garlic, herbs and spices and the beaten egg. Add salt and freshly ground black pepper.

2 Using your hands, shape the mixture into 8 balls. Mould the balls around skewers to form sausage shapes.

3 Place on a hot barbecue until browned all over and cooked through.

4 Combine all the chilli dip ingredients and place in a small serving bowl.

5 Serve the lamb koftas straight from the barbecue with the dipping sauce.

Sticky pork and pineapple kebabs

Makes 4 kebabs
1 kebab 287 kcal/6g fat
Preparation time 30 minutes
Cooking time 30 minutes

4 × 175g (4 × 6oz) lean pork
  steaks
1 medium pineapple
4 tbsps dry sherry
2 tbsps runny honey
2 tbsps Chinese plum sauce
1 tbsp tomato purée
½ tsp caraway seeds
½ tsp five spice powder
2 garlic cloves, finely chopped
zest and juice of 1 lemon
salt and freshly ground black
  pepper

1 Remove all the fat from the pork steaks with a sharp knife and cut into bite-sized pieces. Place in a shallow container.

2 Using a sharp knife, cut off the top and bottom of the pineapple.

3 Standing the fruit on the cut end, slice away the outer skin, cutting in strips from top to bottom around the outside.

4 Using a small knife, cut away any remaining black 'eyes' or small dark pieces of skin.

5 Slice the pineapple into 4 quarters and remove the central core.

6 Slice each quarter in half lengthways, then cut into 2.5cm (1in) pieces.

7 Combine the remaining ingredients in a small bowl and mix well, seasoning with pepper (but not salt).

8 Thread alternate pieces of pork and pineapple up to the handle on metal skewers or leaving 5cm (2in) from the end of wooden ones.

9 Place on a baking tray, brush the marinade over the pork and turn over the kebabs, coating both sides thoroughly.

10 Cover with food wrap and refrigerate until ready to cook. Allow at least 30 minutes for the marinade to permeate the meat. Before cooking, remove from the refrigerator and season with salt.

11 Cook on a hot barbecue for 8–10 minutes on each side, basting with more glaze if required. Serve piping hot with a selection of salads.

Lamb kebabs with apricot and smoked garlic

A very simple way of serving lean lamb. Try to cut the meat into
uniform-sized slices to ensure it cooks evenly.

Serves 4
1 serving 366 kcal/18g fat
Preparation time 10 minutes
Cooking time 45 minutes

1kg (2lb) lean lamb (ideally leg)
2 smoked garlic cloves, sliced
1 tbsp chopped fresh mixed
**   herbs**
2 tbsps apricot jam
1 tbsp light soy sauce
salt and freshly ground black
**   pepper**

1 Trim away any traces of fat from the lamb
and slice into thin strips.

2 Take 8 wooden kebab skewers and carefully thread 2–3 pieces of meat
onto each skewer. Season generously with salt and black pepper.

3 In a small bowl mix together the garlic, herbs, jam and soy sauce. Using
a pastry brush, lightly coat both sides of the meat with the glaze.

4 Place over a hot barbecue and cook for 5–6 minutes on each side.
Brush with the glaze during cooking to
prevent the meat from drying out.

5 Serve with
mixed salads.

Wooden skewers
Cheap to buy and handy to use,
wooden skewers can be cut down to
size easily with kitchen scissors.
Soaking wooden skewers in cold water
for 1 hour before threading with food
will help to prevent the exposed wood
from burning during cooking.

Metal skewers
Many designs offer an attractive way of
presenting kebabs. Being metal, they
will conduct the heat from the
barbecue, so take care when serving. As
with all skewers, the pointed end
requires to be extremely sharp in order
to pierce the meat when threading, so
take care both in preparation and
serving, especially with young children.

OTHER KEBAB COMBINATIONS

A Sirlion steak and baby mushrooms

B Chilli prawns

C Chicken and diced peppers

D Salmon and monkfish

E Lamb with dried, soaked or fresh apricots

F Baby vegetables

Spicy fresh marlin and pepper kebabs

Fresh marlin has a dense meaty texture, similar to fresh tuna but less expensive! It makes a good substantial meal and is low in calories and fat. It can be served slightly rare, as overcooking may lead to a dry texture. You can substitute fresh tuna for marlin if you prefer.

Serves 4
1 serving 264 kcal/8g fat
Preparation time 25 minutes
Cooking time 10 minutes

4 fresh marlin steaks (approx. 175g/6oz each)
1 red and 1 yellow pepper

for the marinade
4 tbsps light soy sauce
zest and juice of 2 limes
1 small red chilli, seeded and finely chopped
1 × 2.5cm (1in) piece fresh ginger, peeled and finely chopped
1 tbsp tomato purée
salt and freshly ground black pepper

1 Remove any skin from the marlin steaks and cut into 5cm (2in) pieces.

2 Slice the sides off the peppers with a sharp knife and cut into large dice.

3 Thread 8 wooden skewers with alternate pieces of marlin and pepper and place in a shallow dish.

4 Combine all the marinade ingredients in a small bowl and pour over the kebabs. Leave to marinate for 20 minutes.

5 Cook the kebabs on a hot barbecue for 4–5 minutes on each side. If overcooked, the texture will become tough and rubbery.

Griddled tuna with coriander and lime pesto

Pesto is usually made with olive oil and pine nuts, both being high in fat. Try this no-fat version which uses fresh coriander instead of fresh basil.

Serves 4
1 serving 248 kcal/8.1g fat
Preparation time 25 minutes
Cooking time 10 minutes

4 fresh tuna steaks
salt and freshly ground black
**   pepper**

for the pesto
zest and juice of 2 limes
4 tbsps light soy sauce
1 garlic clove, crushed
good bunch of fresh coriander
1 tsp ground coriander
salt and freshly ground black
**   pepper**

Place the tuna steaks in a shallow dish. Season well on both sides with salt and black pepper.

Using a zester, remove thin strips of zest from the lime and add to a food processor along with the juice. Add the remaining ingredients and blend until smooth.

Cook the tuna quickly over a hot barbecue for 4–5 minutes on each side. If overcooked, the texture will become tough and rubbery.

Once cooked, place on a hot serving plate and drizzle with the pesto.

Serve hot with salad leaves or vegetables drizzled with fruit vinegar.

Charcoal pork slices with barbecue sauce

Serve these spice-crusted steaks with a rich barbecue sauce and a simple salad selection.

Serves 4
1 serving 267 kcal/7g fat
Preparation time 10 minutes
Cooking time 20 minutes

4 lean pork steaks
1 tbsp sesame seeds
1 tbsp paprika
1 tbsp ground coriander
salt and freshly ground black
**   pepper**

for the barbecue sauce
300ml (½ pint) tomato passata
6 spring onions, finely chopped
2 smoked garlic cloves, crushed
2 tbsps reduced-salt soy sauce
zest and juice of 1 lemon
1 tsp smoked paprika
2 tsps caster sugar
½ tsp caraway seeds (optional)

1 Remove any fat from the pork steaks and season on both sides with a little salt and black pepper.

2 Mix together the sesame seeds and spices on a large plate. Press the pork slices into the spices to coat both sides.

3 Place on the barbecue and cook, turning regularly, for 15–20 minutes, depending on the thickness of the slices. Test if cooked by cutting a pork slice in half.

4 Combine all the sauce ingredients and pour into a serving bowl.

5 Serve the pork slices hot and drizzle the barbecue sauce on top.

Smokey tomato sauce

This simple sauce is so easy to make. To add a fruity flavour, mix in 115g (4oz) fresh blueberries at the beginning and cook in the same way.

Serves 6
1 serving (including blueberries)
    32 kcal/0.3g fat
Preparation time 5 minutes
Cooking time 15 minutes

1 red onion, sliced
2 garlic cloves, crushed
300ml (½ pint) tomato passata
2 tbsps Worcestershire sauce
1 small red chilli, finely sliced
2 tbsps balsamic vinegar
1 tbsp runny honey
1 tsp Dijon mustard
1 tsp smoked paprika
salt and freshly ground
    black pepper

1 Place all the ingredients into a small saucepan and slowly bring to the boil.

2 Simmer gently for 15 minutes until the onion is soft. Serve hot or cold.

Green chilli salsa

A salsa is a chunky accompaniment, ideal to serve with meat and fish.
For a creamy salsa add 2–3 tbsps of low-fat natural yogurt.

Serves 6
1 serving 21 kcal/0.1g fat
Preparation time 10 minutes

2 limes
2 Granny Smith eating apples
2 green peppers, seeded and
**   diced**
½ cucumber, diced
1–2 green chillies, seeded and
**   finely chopped**
good handful of chopped fresh
**   coriander leaves**
salt and freshly ground black
**   pepper**

1 Zest and juice the limes into a bowl.

2 Cut the apples into quarters and remove the core with a small knife. Dice into small pieces and add to the lime. Stir well to coat the apple and prevent it from turning brown.

3 Add the remaining ingredients and mix well, seasoning with salt and black pepper. Spoon into a serving bowl and chill until required.

Jacket potatoes

Jacket potatoes are great cooked over a barbecue. After scrubbing the potatoes, use a fork to pierce well, all over the skin of each potato. Season well with salt, then wrap individually in kitchen foil and place directly onto the heat. Depending on the size of the potatoes on a hot barbecue, allow approximately 1 hour to cook fully. (See page 196 for tasty fillings.)

Each potato, approximately 175g (6oz), 228 kcal/0.6g fat

Easy vegetables

Many vegetables can be cooked directly on the barbecue with very little preparation. Here are some examples:

Peppers Cut peppers in half and remove the centre seeds. Place directly onto the heat, seasoning as you cook.

Mushrooms Choose large, flat mushrooms, wipe clean and remove the centre stalk. Season well and cook directly on the heat.

Beef tomatoes These require very little cooking. Slice in half across the fruit, season and cook.

Courgette and aubergine Slice thickly and season generously. Turn regularly during cooking.

Sweetcorn Cook the corn first in boiling water containing a vegetable stock cube. Drain and place on the barbecue for added flavour.

Barbecue desserts

Barbecue honey bananas

Serves 4
1 serving 191 kcal/0.4g fat
Preparation time 10 minutes
Cooking time 5 minutes

4 medium ripe bananas
1 large orange
1 tbsp stem ginger in syrup
3 tbsps runny honey
3 tbsps demerara sugar

1 Using a small knife, split along the length of each banana skin, pull the skin apart slightly and place on a non-stick baking tray.

2 Using a zester, zest the orange peel into a small bowl.

3 Cut the orange in half and squeeze out the juice. Drain the syrup from the ginger into the bowl and finely chop the ginger and add along with the honey.

4 Mix together well then, pulling the skin apart, spoon onto the bananas.

5 Sprinkle with demerara sugar and wrap each banana in a piece of kitchen foil.

6 Place immediately on a hot barbecue for 5–6 minutes until the bananas are soft. Serve piping hot with virtually fat-free fromage frais.

FRUIT KEBABS

Fresh fruit is the perfect quick and easy option for a barbecue dessert. When barbecuing fruit, choose firm fruits that will hold together after being exposed to high temperatures. Dusting the fruits with icing sugar while they are cooking adds a caramelised flavour.

Fresh lime cheesecake

This rich, lime cheesecake makes a fantastic centrepiece. You can make it in advance and keep in the refrigerator until required.

Serves 8
1 serving 228 kcal/0.7g fat
Preparation time 20 minutes
Cooking time 5 minutes

220g sponge flan case
4 large limes
6 sheets leaf gelatine
1 × 405g can light condensed milk, chilled overnight
1 vanilla pod
200g (7oz) virtually fat-free fromage frais
250g (9oz) Quark (low-fat soft cheese)
2 egg whites
fresh berries and icing sugar to decorate

1 Lightly grease an adjustable flan ring; then press it into the sponge case, just inside the outside edge. Remove the outside edge and discard. Line the ring with parchment paper.

2 Finely grate the lime zest from all 4 limes into a mixing bowl and add the condensed milk.

3 Using an electric mixer, whisk on high speed until thick and double in volume.

4 Soak the gelatine in cold water, then drain, squeezing out any excess water from the gelatine.

5 Cut the limes in half and squeeze out the juice into a small saucepan. Split the vanilla pod lengthways, using a sharp knife, and scrape out the black seeds from the centre.

6 Add the vanilla seeds and the gelatine to the pan. Heat gently, stirring continuously, until the gelatine has dissolved.

7 Whisk the hot syrup into the milk until fully combined. Carefully fold in the fromage frais and Quark until smooth.

8 Whisk the egg whites until they form stiff peaks. Fold into the mixture, using a large metal spoon, and then pour into the ring.

9 Refrigerate for 4 hours, ideally overnight, until set.

10 Decorate with fresh berries and dust with icing sugar before serving.

Christmas

Christmas is the perfect occasion to celebrate with family and friends – and what better way to do it than with food! At this time of year we are always on the search for that easy recipe that takes very little time to prepare yet leaves everyone speechless at the dinner table.

These recipes may not be the quickest but they certainly will impress, and your family and guests won't even guess that they are low in fat. Now that you have adapted your everyday cooking to low fat, use your new-found talents to produce a memorable festive feast.

This chapter includes a selection of recipes from simple starters, traditional turkey and accompaniments, Christmas ham and a fabulous vegetarian option, to a celebratory Christmas pudding that looks and tastes great.

Starters

Melon boat

Serves 4
1 serving 44 kcal/0.1g fat
Preparation time 5 minutes

1 Cut a melon into quarters.

2 Using a serrated knife, cut away the flesh from the skin, then make one cut along the length and several cuts across the melon boat. Serve with orange slices.

Melon basket

Serves 2
1 serving 58 kcal/0.3g fat
Preparation time 5 minutes

1 Take a melon and, using a melon baller, press it into the flesh of the melon and turn to extract equal-sized balls of melon.

2 Place in a glass dish. Alternatively, using a small serrated knife, cut into a whole melon and use as a serving bowl.

3 For a more decadent starter add 2–3 tsps of port just before serving.

Quick prawn cocktail

Serves 6
1 serving 121 kcal/12.9g fat
Preparation time 10 minutes

1 little gem lettuce, shredded
450g (1lb) shelled prawns,
   washed
3 tbsps tomato ketchup
3 tbsps reduced-oil salad
   dressing
dash of Tabasco sauce
salt and freshly ground black
   pepper
pinch of paprika
6 whole king prawns and lemon
   slices to garnish

1 Place the shredded lettuce in 6 small dishes and arrange the prawns on top.

2 Combine the tomato ketchup and salad dressing in a small bowl, and season to taste with salt and pepper and a dash of Tabasco.

3 Spoon the dressing over the prawns and sprinkle with paprika.

4 Sprinkle the paprika on top and garnish with the king prawns and lemon slices.

Main courses

Orange and honey glazed gammon

A truly delicious way to prepare and serve Christmas ham. Should you find gammon too salty, place the gammon in a large bowl of cold water, cover and refrigerate overnight. This will draw out some of the salt. Rinse well in cold water before cooking.

Serves 6
1 serving 582 kcal/15g fat
Preparation time 20 minutes
Cooking time 1 hour 35 minutes

- 1 × 2kg (4lb) piece lean boiling bacon or gammon
- 3 oranges, sliced
- 2 star anise
- 6 whole cloves
- 2 cinnamon sticks
- 4 bay leaves
- 3 tbsps traditional thick-cut orange marmalade
- 1 tbsp runny honey
- 2 tsps demerera sugar

1 Preheat the oven to 180C, 350F, Gas Mark 5.

2 Prepare the gammon by removing all the outer skin and fat with a sharp knife. Place in a large saucepan and cover with cold water. Add the orange slices, anise, cloves, cinnamon and bay leaves. Bring the pan to the boil, cover and simmer gently for 1 hour.

3 Transfer the gammon to an ovenproof dish, and pour some of the stock around to prevent it from sticking to the bottom of the dish.

4 Mix together the marmalade and honey. Coat the meat with the mixture and bake in the oven, uncovered, for 20–25 minutes until golden brown.

5 Sprinkle the gammon with sugar and return to the oven for 5–10 minutes until caramelised.

6 Allow to cool, then garnish with slices of fresh fruit.

7 Serve sliced cold with fruit chutney and salads.

Twice-baked goats' cheese soufflé with roast red peppers

These delicious soufflés make a festive vegetarian main course feast. You can make them in advance and freeze them and then cook straight from the freezer. Allow 15–20 minutes cooking time from frozen.

Serves 4
1 serving 187 kcal/8.7g fat
Preparation time 10 minutes
Cooking time 45 minutes

300ml (½ pint) skimmed milk
1 tsp vegetable stock powder
1 garlic clove, crushed
2 tsps Dijon mustard
1 tbsp cornflour
150g (5oz) fresh soft goats' cheese
2 eggs, separated
1 tbsp finely chopped fresh chives
pinch of cayenne pepper
2 red peppers, seeded
black pepper

1 Preheat the oven to 200C, 400F, Gas Mark 6. Lightly grease 4 large ramekins or ovenproof bowls with spray oil.

2 Heat the milk, stock, garlic and mustard in a non-stick saucepan. Slake the cornflour with a little cold milk and add to the pan, stirring continuously, and bring to the boil. Reduce the heat and simmer for 4–5 minutes to thicken the sauce.

3 Remove from the heat and beat in the goats' cheese. Allow to cool slightly, then beat in the egg yolks one at a time. Add the chives and season with cayenne pepper.

4 Whisk the egg whites with an electric whisk until they form stiff peaks then carefully fold into the sauce, using a metal spoon. Once combined, pour into the prepared bowls and level off with a palette knife.

5 Bake in the middle of the oven for 20 minutes until well risen and brown. Remove from the oven and leave to cool.

6 Meanwhile cut the red peppers into strips and place in a non-stick roasting tin. Roast in the oven for 20 minutes until lightly charred.

7 Run a small knife around the edge of each bowl and turn out the soufflés on to a baking tray – they can be wrapped and frozen at this point.

8 Bake the soufflés, uncovered, for 10 minutes until golden brown and puffy. Serve immediately with a few salad leaves and the roasted pepper strips.

Roast turkey with giblet gravy

Serves 10
1 serving 200 kcal/4g fat
Preparation time 40 minutes
Cooking time 3½ hours

**1 × 5.4 kg (12lb) fresh or
defrosted turkey with giblets
1 large onion, diced
2 carrots, sliced
4–5 sprigs fresh thyme
pinch of sea salt
freshly ground black pepper
2–3 tsps gravy granules**

1 Preheat the oven to 180C, 350F, Gas Mark 5. Calculate the cooking time, allowing 15 minutes per 450g (1lb) plus an extra 20 minutes.

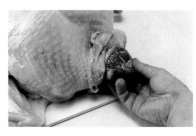

2 Wash the turkey well in cold water and remove the neck from the top of the bird and any excess fat.

3 Remove the giblets, which will be in a plastic bag at the base of the bird, and reserve.

4 Rinse the turkey well under cold running water, allowing the water to flush through the bird.

5 Prepare a large roasting tray by placing the chopped vegetables and giblets in the centre. Place a roasting rack over and pour 600ml (1 pint) of water into the tray.

6 Sit the turkey on top. Pull out the wing tips and twist, tucking them under the bird; this will prevent them from burning during cooking.

7 Season the turkey well with salt and freshly ground black pepper. Cover with foil and place in the oven.

8 Split the total cooking time into three, turning the bird onto its other side after one third of the cooking time and placing it breast-side up for the final third (this will ensure even cooking). Baste the bird with the juices in the bottom of the roasting tray during cooking to keep the bird moist.

9 Once the turkey is cooked, test by using a meat thermometer or by inserting a skewer into the thickest part of the turkey through the thigh. The juices should run clear without traces of blood. If in any doubt return the turkey to the oven and cook for a further 30 minutes and test again. When done, the temperature should be above 75C, 170F.

10 Remove from the roasting tray and place on a serving dish. Keep it covered with foil and allow 30 minutes standing time for easier carving.

11 Drain the contents of the roasting tray into a bowl. Remove the giblets and bay leaf and discard.

12 Add 6 ice cubes to help congeal the fat, then use a ladle to skim off any fat from the top of the bowl or pour into a gravy separator.

13 Pour off the meat juices into a saucepan. Heat, adding more water if required, and thicken with 2–3 tsps of gravy granules, stirring well to prevent lumps from forming.

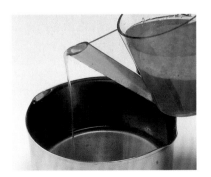

CARVING THE TURKEY

1 Remove the leg by slicing down in between the leg joint and the carcass.

2 Cut the leg from the thigh where the natural joint runs.

3 Slice the breast meat from one side of the breast and across the top, taking alternate slices.

4 Finish slicing the whole side, then repeat on the other side.

BACON ROLLS

These are a tasty and traditional accompaniment to roast turkey. Sausages and bacon can vary considerably in fat content, so be very selective and choose half-fat sausages and the leanest of bacon. Simply wrap thin straps of bacon around each sausage and place on a non-stick baking tray. Bake in a preheated oven (180C, 350F, Gas Mark 5) for 35 minutes until golden brown. Slice in half.

Vegetable side dishes

Fat-free roast potatoes and parsnips

Serves 6
1 serving 106 kcal/0.9g fat
Preparation time 20 minutes
Cooking time 60 minutes

450g (1lb) potatoes, peeled
8 medium parsnips, peeled and left whole
2 vegetable stock cubes
1 tbsp soy sauce diluted in 2 tbsps of water (optional)

1 Preheat the oven to 200C, 400F, Gas Mark 6. Cut the potatoes in half and trim the tops from the parsnips.

2 Cook the potatoes and parsnips separately in boiling water containing the stock cubes for 5 minutes. Drain.

3 Place in separate non-stick roasting tins and baste with the diluted soy sauce if desired.

4 Place in the top of the oven for 35-40 minutes for parsnips and 60 minutes for potatoes until golden brown. You can baste the vegetables with the diluted soy sauce if they appear to dry out.

Brussels sprouts with pancetta

Adding a few extras to vegetables transforms them, adding texture and a contrast of flavours. For a vegetarian option you can use veggie bacon slices instead of pancetta and cook in the same way.

Serves 4
1 serving 116 kcal/7g fat
Preparation time 20 minutes
Cooking time 20 minutes

450g (1lb) Brussels sprouts
1 vegetable stock cube
**4 slices pancetta or smoked
    streaky bacon**
**salt and freshly ground black
    pepper**

1 Remove the loose outer leaves from the sprouts, using a small paring knife.

2 Make a small nick in the form of a cross in the stalks.

3 Cook in boiling water with the stock until just tender.

4 Chop the pancetta or bacon into small pieces.

CARROTS

Adding a tsp of cumin seeds as well as a vegetable stock cube to the water during cooking adds a lovely flavour to cooked carrots.

5 Preheat a non-stick pan. Add the pancetta or bacon.

6 Dry-fry for 3–4 minutes until crisp, then remove from the pan and place on kitchen paper.

7 Wipe out the pan with kitchen paper.

8 Return the pancetta to the pan, add the cooked, drained Brussels sprouts and mix well.

9 Season with salt and pepper. Spoon into a serving dish and keep warm until ready to serve.

Sauces and stuffings

Chestnut stuffing

Serves 8
1 serving 85 kcal/0.8g fat
Preparation time 25 minutes
Cooking time 20–25 minutes

1 medium onion, finely chopped
1 garlic clove, crushed
115g (4oz) fresh breadcrumbs
1 tbsp finely chopped fresh
  thyme
1 tbsp chopped fresh parsley
115g (4oz) peeled chestnuts,
  finely chopped
1 tsp finely grated lemon zest
300ml (½ pint) hot chicken stock
black pepper to taste

1 Preheat the oven to 180C, 350F, Gas Mark 4.

2 Place the onion, garlic, breadcrumbs and herbs in a mixing bowl. Add the chestnuts and lemon zest. Pour in the chicken stock and allow to stand for 10 minutes.

3 Mould into golf-ball-sized pieces and place on a non-stick baking tray.

4 Bake in the oven for 20–25 minutes until brown and crisp.

Low-fat bread sauce

Serves 8
1 serving 41 kcal/0.2g fat
Preparation time 10 minutes
Cooking time 25 minutes

300ml (½ pint) skimmed milk
1 small onion, chopped
3 cloves
1 bay leaf
6–8 tbsps fresh breadcrumbs
salt and freshly ground black
**   pepper**

1 Slowly bring the milk to the boil and add the chopped onion, cloves and bay leaf.

2 Remove from the heat, cover the pan and leave on one side for 15–20 minutes to allow the flavours to infuse.

3 When infused, remove the cloves and bay leaf, add the breadcrumbs and black pepper and return to the heat, stirring gently until the mixture comes to the boil. Season with salt and black pepper.

4 Remove from the heat and place in a small covered serving dish (a small bowl covered with aluminium foil would work just as well). Keep warm until ready to serve.

Puddings, cakes and sweet treats

Low-fat Christmas pudding

This simple pudding is so easy to make and it tastes even better than the traditional ones. Steaming gives a nicer, moister pudding but the microwave method is also good. If you wish, you can soak the fruit in the brandy rum or beer and leave overnight.

Serves 10
1 serving 280 kcal/2.5g fat
Preparation time 20 minutes
Cooking time
Microwave 15–20 minutes
Steaming 5 hours

75g (3oz) currants
75g (3oz) sultanas
115g (4oz) raisins
75g (3oz) glacé cherries, halved
75g (3oz) plain or self-raising
   flour
1 tsp mixed spice
½ tsp ground cinnamon
50g (2oz) fresh breadcrumbs
50g (2oz) brown sugar
2 tsps gravy browning
grated zest of ½ lemon
grated zest of ½ orange
115g (4oz) grated apple
115g (4oz) carrots, finely grated
4 tbsps brandy, rum or beer
1 tbsp lemon juice
2 eggs, beaten
4 tbsps skimmed milk
2 tbsps molasses or cane sugar
   syrup
extra 4 tbsps rum or brandy for
   reheating

1 Combine all the dry ingredients and all the wet ingredients in 2 separate bowls. Mix together and add the beaten egg.

2 Continue mixing until all the ingredients are combined.

3 Pour the mixture into a 1.2 litre (2 pint) pudding basin or glass bowl and cover with aluminium foil if steaming (not if microwaving).

4 Place in a steamer and cook, covered, for 3 hours.

5 If microwaving the pudding, place an upturned plate over the basin and microwave on full power for 5 minutes. Leave to stand for 5 minutes, then microwave for a further 5 minutes.

6 After cooking, allow the pudding to cool, then wrap in aluminium foil and leave in a cool, dry place until required.

7 To reheat the pudding, steam for 1–2 hours or microwave for 10 minutes.

8 When cooked, run a knife round the edge of the basin, turn out onto a serving plate and drizzle with brandy or rum. Serve with low-fat brandy sauce (see recipe).

CHEF'S TIP

Make this Christmas pudding a month in advance to maximise the flavours. Drizzle with 1 tbsp of brandy or rum each week leading up to Christmas. Store in an airtight container. Reheat as in stage 7 and serve with a low-fat brandy sauce.

Low-fat brandy sauce

Makes 600ml (1 pint)
Per 600ml (1 pint) 386 kcal/0.9g fat
Preparation time 5 minutes
Cooking time 15 minutes

600ml (1 pint) skimmed milk
3 drops almond essence
2 tbsps cornflour
liquid artificial sweetener
3 tbsps brandy

1 Heat all but 4 tbsps of the milk with the almond essence until almost boiling and remove from the heat.

2 Mix the cornflour and remaining cold milk thoroughly and slowly pour it into the hot milk, stirring continuously until the mixture begins to thicken.

3 Return the pan to the heat and bring the mixture to the boil. Continue to cook, stirring all the time. If the consistency is too thin, mix some more cornflour with cold milk and add it slowly until you achieve the consistency of custard. Sweeten to taste.

4 Add the brandy a few drops at a time and stir well. Place in a serving jug, cover and keep warm until ready to serve.

Filo pastry mince pies

Makes 6 mince pies
1 mince pie 144 kcal/1.5g fat
Preparation time 20 minutes
Cooking time 10 minutes

6 sheets filo pastry (30cm × 20cm/12in × 8in)
1 egg white, beaten
3 tbsps spicy fat-free mincemeat (recipe, page 274)
icing sugar to decorate (optional)

1 Preheat the oven to 190C, 375F, Gas Mark 5. Lightly grease a non-stick mince pie or patty tin for easy removal of the finished pies, which will be very fragile.

2 Stack the filo pastry sheets on top of each other on the work surface. Using scissors, cut the stack into 6 square-shaped sections, so that you end up with 36 individual squares. Keep moist.

3 Fill each mould by placing 4 individual pastry squares in layers, placing the squares at slight angles to each other and brushing with beaten egg white in between each layer.

4 Place a half tablespoonful of mincemeat in the centre of each pastry case.

5 Brush the remaining 12 pastry squares with egg white and scrunch them up to make crinkly toppings for the pies. Place 2 scrunched-up squares on top of each portion of mincemeat.

6 Bake in the oven for 10 minutes until the pastry is crisp and golden. Just before serving, dust with a little icing sugar (if using).

Spicy fat-free mincemeat

Makes 450g (1lb)
450g (1lb) 775 kcal/1.1g fat

150g (5oz) cooking apples,
  grated
225g (8oz) mixed dried fruit
½ tsp mixed spice
150ml (¼ pint) sweet cider
2 tbsps brandy, whisky or rum

1 Place the grated apples and the dried fruit in a saucepan. Add the mixed spice and cider. Simmer for about 20 minutes or until the mixture forms a pulp and most of the liquid has evaporated.

2 Stir in your choice of spirit. Allow to cool.

3 When cool, pack the mincemeat in sterilised jars and store in the refrigerator until required. The mincemeat will keep in a refrigerator for 4 months. Once opened, use within one week.

Christmas meringue

This is a delicious variation of mincemeat tart. The fat content has been considerably reduced to allow for the light meringue topping.

Serves 8
1 serving 246 kcal/1.8g fat
Preparation time 20 minutes
Cooking time 60 minutes

for the flan base
2 eggs
75g (3oz) golden caster sugar
75g (3oz) self raising flour,
   sifted
1 tsp vanilla essence

for the filling
1 cooking apple, grated
225g (8oz) dried luxury fruits
1 tsp mixed spice
150ml (¼ pint) fresh orange
   juice
2 tbsps brandy

for the topping
2 egg whites
115g (4oz) caster sugar

1 Preheat the oven to 180C, 350F, Gas Mark 4.

2 Grease a 20cm (8in) non-stick flan case with a little vegetable oil, then dust with caster sugar.

3 To make the sponge base, whisk together the eggs and sugar for several minutes until thick and pale in consistency. Using a metal spoon, fold in the sifted flour and then the vanilla.

4 Pour into the prepared flan case and level off with a knife. Bake in the oven for 20 minutes until golden brown.

5 Allow the sponge to cool then, using a serrated knife, cut away a 1cm (½in) layer of sponge from the centre of the flan case. Using a metal spoon, scrape away the crumbs to leave a smooth surface.

6 Place the grated apple and fruit in a small saucepan. Add the spice and liquid.

7 Simmer gently until the fruit plumps up and most of the liquid has been absorbed. Allow to cool, then spoon into the sponge filling.

8 Whisk the egg whites until stiff. Still whisking, add the caster sugar one dessertspoon at a time, leaving 10 seconds between each addition, until all the sugar is used. Place the meringue into a piping bag and pipe across the top of the flan. Return to the oven for 20 minutes or until golden brown.

9 Serve hot or cold with fresh orange segments.

Low-fat Christmas cake

Cakes made without the use of butter or margarine have a very different texture, probably best described as slightly chewy. They do however taste less greasy and more fruity. This cake benefits from being made at least one week in advance.

Makes approximately 20 slices
Per slice 228 kcal/2.8g fat
Preparation time 30 minutes
Cooking time 2–2½ hours

225g (8oz) no pre-soak prunes,
  pitted
115g (4oz) cooking apple,
  grated
175g (6oz) dark muscovado
  sugar
4 eggs, beaten
1 lemon and 1 orange, zested
175g (6oz) self-raising flour,
  sifted
1 tbsp mixed spice
50g (2oz) sunflower seeds
225g (8oz) currants
225g (8oz) sultanas
225g (8oz) raisins
115g (4oz) glacé cherries
120ml (4fl oz) brandy
2 tbsps apricot jam, sieved, to
  glaze

1 Preheat the oven to 170C, 325F, Gas Mark 3. Lightly grease and line a round cake tin (20cm/8in in diameter, 7.5cm/3in deep) with greaseproof paper.

2 In a large mixing bowl mix together the prunes and apple. Add the sugar, then beat in the eggs a little at a time.

3 Press down the mixture to squash the prunes.

4 Mix in the lemon and orange zest, then carefully fold in the flour, spice, sunflower seeds and fruit.

5 Gradually stir in the brandy.

6 Pour into the prepared cake tin.

7 Using the back of a metal spoon, make a slight dip in the centre to allow for an even top once baked. Bake in the oven for 2-2½ hours or until a metal skewer inserted into the cake comes out clean.

8 Allow to cool on a wire rack, then remove the greaseproof paper. Glaze by brushing with warmed apricot jam and arrange some cherries or dried fruits on top. Store in an airtight container.

Peach, pear and cinnamon trifle

Serves 6
1 serving 193 kcal/0.7g fat
Preparation time 10 minutes
Cooking time 10 minutes

4 ripe peaches
2 ripe pears
2 tsps ground cinnamon
2 sherry glasses sweet sherry
1 packet sugar-free jelly
1 × 425g carton low-fat custard
1 vanilla pod
300g (11oz) 0% fat Greek
   yogurt
2 cinnamon sticks

This gives a slight twist on this traditional festive dessert.
Choose ripe fruits, as these will yield the maximum flavour.

1   Prepare the fruit by cutting the peaches in half and removing the centre stones. Chop into slices and place in a small saucepan. Peel the pears and cut into quarters lengthways. Chop into small pieces and add to the saucepan.

2   Add 1 tsp of ground cinnamon, along with the sherry, and place the saucepan over a low heat to soften the fruit.

3   Make up the jelly according to the packet instructions, reducing the water by 120ml (4floz) to allow for the sherry.

4   When the fruits are soft, arrange in the bottom of a glass bowl, reserving a few slices for the top. Pour the jelly over the top and refrigerate until set, preferably overnight.

5   When set, cover with the low-fat custard.

6   Place the vanilla pod onto a chopping board. Using the point of a sharp knife, split the pod down the centre lengthways. Run the blade of the knife along the pod, scraping out the vanilla seeds. Add the seeds to the yogurt, along with the remaining cinnamon, and mix well.

7   Spoon the yogurt over the top of the custard and smooth with a knife. Decorate with the reserved fruit slices.

CHRISTMAS FRUITS

At one time, Christmas for some would mean maybe the odd tangerine or satsuma in their festive stocking. Now we have limitless opportunities to dress our tables with more exotic varieties of fruit. Here are a few suggestions to enjoy them at their best.

Kumquats These tiny miniature oranges can be eaten whole or lightly stewed in red wine or port. Delicious mixed with quarters of fresh figs.

Physalis (also named Cape Gooseberry) These bright orange berries wrapped in a papery husk are ideal for using as a garnish or served with drinks instead of high-fat olives or nuts. They have a very unusual flavour, so do give them a try.

Blueberries, bilberries and cranberries These are all in season together. Cranberries are sour in flavour compared to the other two sweet berries, so the solution is to mix them together to make a fruit compote or blended sauce to serve alongside vegetables, fish and meat.

Index